MAKING WIRE & BEAD JEWELRY

■ ARTFUL WIREWORK TECHNIQUES ■

JANICE BERKEBILE & TRACY STANLEY

LARK CRAFTS
Asheville

editor
Nathalie Mornu

editorial assistance
Dawn Dillingham
Hannah Doyle
Abby Haffelt

art directors
Kathleen Holmes
Carol Morse Barnao

project photographer
Stewart O'Shields

how-to photographers
Janice Berkebile
Tracy Stanley

book designer
Laura Palese

editorial intern
Virginia M. Roper

LARK CRAFTS

An Imprint of Sterling Publishing
387 Park Avenue South
New York, NY 10016

If you have questions or comments about
this book, please visit larkcrafts.com.

Library of Congress Cataloging-in-Publication Data

Berkebile, Janice, 1959-
  Making wire & bead jewelry : artful wirework techniques / Janice Berkebile &
Tracy Stanley.—1st ed.
    p. cm.
  ISBN 978-1-4547-0287-0 (pbk.)
  1. Jewelry making. 2. Wire jewelry. 3. Beadwork. I. Stanley, Tracy, 1955- II. Title.
  III. Title: Making wire and bead jewelry.
  TT212.B49 2012
  739.27—dc23

                    2011037354

10 9 8 7 6 5 4 3 2 1

First Edition
Published by Lark Crafts
An Imprint of Sterling Publishing Co., Inc.
387 Park Avenue South, New York, NY 10016

Text © 2012, Janice Berkebile and Tracy Stanley
Photography © 2012, Lark Crafts, an Imprint of Sterling Publishing Co., Inc., unless
otherwise specified
How-to photography © 2012, Janice Berkebile and Tracy Stanley
Illustrations © 2012, Lark Crafts, an Imprint of Sterling Publishing Co., Inc., unless
otherwise specified

Distributed in Canada by Sterling Publishing, c/o Canadian Manda Group,
165 Dufferin Street, Toronto, Ontario, Canada M6K 3H6

Distributed in the United Kingdom by GMC Distribution Services,
Castle Place, 166 High Street, Lewes, East Sussex, England BN7 1XU

Distributed in Australia by Capricorn Link (Australia) Pty Ltd.,
P.O. Box 704, Windsor, NSW 2756 Australia

ISBN 13: 978-1-4547-0287-0

For information about custom editions, special sales, premium, and corporate
purchases, please contact the Sterling Special Sales Department at 800-805-5489 or
specialsales@sterlingpub.com.

Requests for information about desk and examination copies available to college and
university professors must be submitted to academic@larkbooks.com. Our complete
policy can be found at www.larkcrafts.com.

CONTENTS

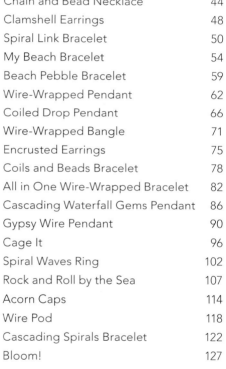

TOOLS & MATERIALS

Wire working has been our passion for many years. Give us some wire and we'll bend it, coil it, wrap it, and forge it into a beautiful piece of jewelry! As we design, we always consider strength, texture, and form. We bend wire with deliberation so that it looks intentional.

Many have asked us how we come up with these designs. For us it's all about solid wire-working skills, quality tools, and practice, practice, and more practice. We've been passing on our skills and knowledge by teaching both locally and on a national level. Our ultimate goal is to send students out in the world of wire working with good solid skills that they can build on and the ability to create amazing pieces that are structurally sound and artfully made. After years of being asked to write a book, we've finally done it!

This chapter gives you a good explanation of the required tools and their proper use—hopefully it will keep you from buying things that won't suit your needs. Then move on to Wire Techniques and really take the time to go over it before jumping into the projects; it will serve you well. Get some inexpensive wire and make the components in that section repeatedly until you can do it well. We can't emphasize this enough. You *don't* want to be practicing on your actual pieces. The more you work with the tools and wire in your hands, the more comfortable you will be with the processes and the easier and more successful they will become. Finally, familiarize yourself with the section on Finishing. Then start making the projects.

We hope you enjoy making and wearing the jewelry in this book as much as we do!

SO, WHAT TOOLS DO YOU NEED?

With wirework, it's all about the tools. Their quality can make or break you. As the old saying goes, you get what you pay for! A good tool will make the learning much easier and if you have problems you'll never have to wonder, "Is it me or the tool?"

Consider getting tools with ergonomic handles; they're much easier on the hands. If higher-end tools are out of your budget, at least

CLOCKWISE FROM TOP LEFT, two styles of round-nose pliers, flat-nose pliers, chain-nose pliers, and flush wire cutters

try to avoid buying tools made in developing countries. In our opinion, these tools are made with low standards from inferior metals.

PLIERS

These tools are extensions of your fingers and the muscles in your hands. You control the tool, and the tool controls the wire.

Round-nose pliers This tool has two round, tapered ends and is used for forming loops. Because of the taper, you can wrap on different places on the pliers' tip to make different-size loops. These pliers come in different lengths. Short ones are more appropriate for working with thinner wire, and long ones are best for heavier gauges.

Multibarrel pliers

Chain-nose pliers The jaws of the chain-nose pliers are flat and smooth on the inside and taper to a point. You'll use this tool like a vise to hold, pull, and bend wire.

Flat-nose pliers These are flat and smooth on the inside and come to a square, blunt end. This tool is used as a second vise and has different leverage points from the chain-nose style. It's also used to form sharp angles in wire.

① shows the difference in the tips of the flat-nose and chain-nose pliers.

Multibarrel pliers These pliers, which come in different sizes, have a round barrel that stair-steps down three or more different sizes. This tool can be used to make jump rings, clasps, and ear wires.

FLUSH WIRE CUTTERS

Flush wire cutters are designed to leave a smooth, flat end when snipping wire. As shown in ②, when closed, flush wire cutters should reveal no channel on the flush side. Be sure to purchase cutters capable of cutting the heaviest gauge of wire you plan on using. We also

SAFETY FIRST!
When cutting wire, wear safety glasses, and always cover the end of the cutter and the wire with one hand, to prevent a small bit of wire from flying into someone's eye.

LEFT, flat-nose pliers; RIGHT, chain-nose pliers

Flush wire cutters

recommend a small fine-tipped pair to use with fine-gauge wire.

You can use the flush wire cutters for the types of wire discussed in the wire section. *Never* use them to cut memory wire.

CHASING HAMMER

A chasing hammer is used to forge wire. Forging will strengthen, spread, and facet wire. The hammer's face should have a slightly domed and smooth finish. (If it's completely flat, it will leave a mark on the wire every time you strike.) The smaller the head, the more control you'll have over where you're striking. You can purchase this type of hammer at jewelry supply stores.

STEEL BENCH BLOCK

You'll use this item to support the wire when you forge it with a chasing hammer. We prefer to use a smooth-surfaced steel block no larger than 3 x 3 inches (7.6 x 7.6 cm), because when you hammer on it, it makes less noise than one of the larger ones, yet still has plenty of surface area. This is another tool you'll find at jewelry supply stores.

BLOCK PAD

This sits under the bench block and helps to deaden the sound of the hammering. It can be as simple as a folded washcloth, a mouse pad, or a commercial pad made out of leather and filled with shot (metal pellets).

FILES

To file sharp wire ends, keep a small metal file or a 1.80-grit emery board on hand. The advantage of emery boards is they have a little give.

MANDRELS

Mandrels are anything you can wind wire around. You can purchase metal mandrels designed specifically for this purpose, or you can use wood dowels or knitting needles. Some mandrels are tapered, but if you get that type, you'll have to watch where you wind on it in order to make a coil that is a consistent size. We prefer to use mandrels that aren't tapered.

METAL HOLE PUNCH

Similar in concept to hand-held hole punches for paper, the ones used for the projects in this book make holes in thicker-gauge wire that has first been flattened. These hole punches come in 1.25 and 1.80 mm. They are sold at jewelry supply stores.

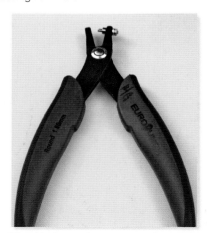

LEFT TO RIGHT, a bench block resting on a leather block pad filled with metal shot, and two chasing hammers.

LEFT, an emery board; RIGHT, a file

Metal hole punch

Mandrels

OPTIONAL TOOLS AND EQUIPMENT

The following tools are things that you may want to consider adding to your toolbox. Many of them are designed to make some processes easier. Although not always necessary, they can make for a nicer finished product.

RING CLAMP

This jeweler's tool holds your coil on the mandrel as you wind, relieving some of the stress on your hand. We don't recommend using a plier to do the job because it crushes the coil and damages the wire. You can buy a ring clamp anywhere jewelers' tools are sold.

JEWELER'S SAW AND BLADES

A jeweler's saw can be used to cut jump rings. This tool will yield the

Ring clamp

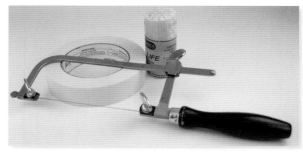

FRONT TO BACK, jeweler's saw, masking tape, and blade conditioner

Ring mandrels

best results because it slices right through so the ends match up perfectly. (When you cut with flush wire cutters, there's always a chance of not getting the ends cut at the exact same angle.) We prefer to use a 3/0-size blade. It has very small teeth, so it cuts smoothly. Running the blade through a blade conditioner before using it will keep it from catching on the wire as you saw. (We don't recommend bee's wax because it tends to gum up the fine teeth.) You can purchase saws, blades, and blade conditioner from any purveyor of jewelers' tools.

RING SIZER

Use this tool to determine the size of ring you want to make. Slide the ring sizer on and adjust it so it

Ring sizer

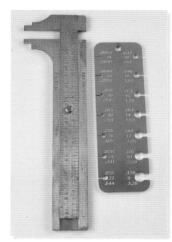

LEFT, caliper; RIGHT, wire gauge. A caliper assesses the size of beads, while the wire gauge measures the diameter, or gauge, of wire. (Learn more about gauge on page 8.) To use this tool, insert the wire into a slot on the edge, looking for a close match. Keep trying smaller and smaller slots until it won't go in. The gauge of the wire is marked on the smallest slot that it fits in.

fits comfortably. See how it has sizes printed on it? The arrow points to the size you want to make your ring.

RING MANDRELS

Ring mandrels are tapered and have ring sizes marked along the length; these correlate with a ring sizer. They're used to form and size a ring. Both wooden and metal ring mandrels exist. We prefer to use a wooden mandrel because it's lighter, but you could use a metal one.

Other tools that you may want to add to your collection would include polishing cloths or pads, a bead scoop, a measuring tape and ruler, and a permanent marker. Use the ruler to measure short pieces of wire, and the tape measure for longer lengths.

A bowl filled with water, a butane torch, and tweezers on a fire-safe surface. The torch is used for making head pins (shown in the foreground) from wire.

HORN ANVIL

This anvil has a hole in the center of it. You can place a spiral head pin down the center of the hole and, with the anvil supporting it, hammer the spiral to work harden and texture it.

BEAD REAMER

When the hole in your bead is too small to allow wire to pass through, you can use a reamer to enlarge the hole.

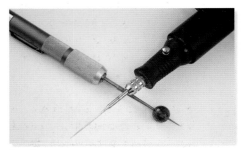

Bead reamers

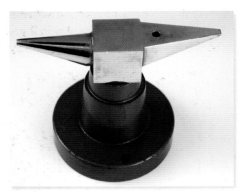

Horn anvil

A reel of brass wire straddles spools holding bronze (on the left) and copper. They're surrounded by various gauges of sterling silver wire.

Some beads made from softer stones, such as turquoise, could be too fragile to ream. You may not find out until you try. The other potential issue with reaming is the shape of the bead. If the bead comes to a tip or is flat in shape, you risk breaking part off. The rule of thumb for reaming is, if you would die if the bead broke, don't do it! Instead, use a thinner wire for your project or choose a different bead.

You can get a manual bead reamer or an electrical one. What types of beads you'll ream, and how much you think you'll use a reamer, may help you make the decision about which sort to purchase. We own both. Both kinds use the same tapered, diamond reamer bits. These come in two sizes; determine the size of the hole you're going to ream to decide which bit is appropriate to use. Learn more on page 27.

WHAT ABOUT THE WIRE?

Wire comes in different metals and different degrees of hardness. As you work with wire, bending and hammering it, it becomes harder and harder. If you start with wire that's in a hard or half-hard state, you may have a tough time manipulating the wire to the shape you desire. So for the most part, we prefer to buy our wire *dead soft*. This means that during its manufacture, the wire has been *annealed* to its softest form. (In the annealing process, the metal is heated, which structurally aligns its molecules so the wire is at its most pliable.)

Wire comes in different diameters, known as *gauge*. The smaller the gauge number, the heavier the wire. The projects in this book call for gauges 12 to 24. We use heavier-

gauge wire for framework and lighter-gauge wire to coil, weave, or embellish.

TIP When you're making any of the projects in this book, feel free to substitute any of the wire—copper can look just as gorgeous as silver—but stick to the recommended gauge.

Each of the different metal wires has its pros and cons.

Sterling silver is actually a combination of silver and copper. It's 92.5% silver, with the rest copper. It's strong and great to work with, but these days it's very pricy. Sterling silver comes in various tempers; dead soft, half hard, or hard. The projects in this book are made from dead-soft wire.

Fine silver is 99% silver. Because of its near purity, it's very soft. We use it to make head pins.

Silver-filled wire has an overlay of sterling silver fused over a brass wire core. It comes in different thicknesses of silver coating, 1/20 and 1/10. (The thicker of the two is 1/10.) This coating is extremely stable and doesn't rub off as on plated wires. The disadvantage of this wire is it's stiffer than the solid sterling, and the brass core can show on the cut ends. The advantage: it costs about half the price of sterling silver.

Gold wire is typically out of reach for many crafters because of its cost. For a suitable substitute, try gold-filled wire. **Gold-filled** wire is gold wire that's bonded with a base metal (a common metal, as opposed to a precious one) to create a finished product that resembles gold. The advantage: the finish doesn't rub off the way it would on a plated wire, and it's more reasonably priced than solid gold.

Copper wire is 100% copper. Copper is an inexpensive wire, and antiquing gives it a beautiful warm tone. The downside is, it's kind of a one-hit wonder: If you get kinks in it, copper wire isn't as easy as silver to smooth out and start over. On the other hand, it's cheap enough that you can use a new piece and not be out a lot of cash.

Brass is also inexpensive, but stiffer than copper and much more so than silver. The other disadvantage to brass is, it requires a special solution to antique. (See page 28 for details.)

Bronze is also an inexpensive wire, compared to silver, but it costs more than copper. It can be harder to find, but it's a beautiful material to use. The biggest disadvantage with bronze is it's extremely hard. It feels at least twice as hard as the other wires described here, and you must be careful with your cutters on this wire. We recommend using only heavy-duty cutters on bronze wire, especially with the heavier gauges.

Plated or colored craft wires are typically inexpensive, but it's often unpredictable how stable the finishes are. We don't recommend using these for finished jewelry, but you can use them to practice.

AND HOW ABOUT BEADS?

Basically, anything with a hole in it can be a bead. Beads come in all shapes and sizes and can be made of just about anything. They can be used as focal elements or as embellishments. Since the world of beads is so vast, we're going to cover our favorites, the ones we always keep on hand. Both of us, no matter the bead type, prefer to use the best quality.

We both love nature and the forms found therein, so some of our favorite beads come straight from the earth. Included in this category are pebbles, shells, pearls, and semi-precious stones.

DRILLED PEBBLES

These most humble of beads are rounded and soothing to the touch. You can buy beach pebbles drilled either through the center or through the top.

SHELLS

These can be purchased with holes already drilled. Tiny shells can be tucked into vessels made with the basket-weave technique, or used for embellishment. Use large shells as focal pieces. Parts of shell are often made into beads. Some of our favorites show off the incredible architecture inside the shell, while others take the form of shimmery faceted beads.

PEARLS

All pearls come from an oyster, but the fabulous array of shades found in the marketplace isn't natural: those are dyed. Our favorites have got to be Tahitian pearls. Grown in the South Seas, they come in a rainbow of colors, all natural. Lovely!

Pearls vary in size from 2 to 14 mm or so. When you're choosing them, test the color for stability by wiping the pearls with a cloth or paper towel. If any of the color comes off, it will also rub off on your clothes and skin if you use those pearls in a piece of jewelry.

Some of these pearls are natural, while others are dyed.

Drilled pebbles

Shells

We love Tahitian pearls!

SEMIPRECIOUS GEMSTONES

This category alone is vast. Some of the varieties of semiprecious beads seen in this book include ruby, green garnet, green amethyst, garnet, amethyst, and charoite, and it goes on and on. Most are available in faceted and non-faceted forms and in all shapes, sizes, and prices. This is another situation where you get what you pay for. Examine the stones you're considering purchasing and check the finishes. Do you see scratches? Irregular coloring? Is the shape uniform? If you're paying top dollar, make sure you're getting top quality.

Semiprecious gemstones

Lampwork beads by Cheryl Sweeney, JoAnne Zekowski, and Barbara Metzger.

LAMPWORK BEADS

These are glass beads made by artisans. You'll find many terrific lampwork bead artists out there.

CRYSTALS

When you need some bling, crystals come in every size, shape, and color imaginable. Add them to your wire and bead jewelry for sparkle and contrast with the wire. Janice includes vintage crystals in the Dog Bone Bracelet (page 34). Tracy used them in My Beach Bracelet (page 54).

SILVER BEADS

Charms, bails, and spacers can all be purchased in solid sterling silver, silver-plated, or base metal. Plated or base metals have finishes that

Crystals

Daisy spacers

will eventually rub off. How long they last will depend on how much contact they have with skin and the elements, so we suggest you purchase sterling silver.

Daisy spacers are basic spacers that can be used all the time. Look for beads cast by silver artisans, too: you'll find bails, charms, and spacers in all shapes and forms.

COMMERCIAL COMPONENTS

Depending on our designs, we sometimes use commercially made components. Chain, jump rings, ear wires, head pins, clasps, and bails are all things you can include in your jewelry. We don't recommend using plated components because the finishes tend to rub off. When purchasing these items, make sure you know what they're made of so you'll be happy with the way they perform in your pieces. Use elements that will hold up over time and do your pieces proud.

These charms were made by one of our favorite silver artisans, Pam Springall.

WIRE TECHNIQUES

This section will teach you the techniques that we use for the projects in the book. Learning and practicing good solid technique will take you far in your wire-working adventures! Take the time to practice—it will be time well spent. Refer back to this section as you make the pieces if you need to brush up.

STRAIGHTENING WIRE

When we come across a kink in wire, we ease it back out using our hands or chain-nose pliers. We don't use commercial wire straighteners. When such a tool is used on 22 or 24 gauge, it work-hardens the metal too much, so the wire becomes brittle and breaks.

MAKING COILS

A coil is a finer gauge of wire that is coiled or wrapped around a larger piece of wire or a mandrel. A coil shouldn't have a lot of gaps or over-laps; instead it should look neat, with each round of coiling right beside the previous one. You can use coiling as an embellishment over a wire armature, the way Janice did in the Gypsy Wire Pendant (page 90); this adds strength and texture. Or you can use a piece of coiled wire just like a bead, like Tracy did in the All in One Wire-Wrapped Bracelet (page 82). Use gauges from 26 to 18 to coil, depending on the scale of your project and the purpose of the coil.

HAND COILING

> ### YOU'LL NEED
> 2 feet (61 cm) of 18-gauge wire
> A mandrel, 3-mm

Start coiling either from the end of the wire or at its center. If you start at the end of the wire, leave a 1-inch (2.5 cm) tail to hold on to. If the wire is exceptionally long, then start in the center of the wire. Coil away from yourself because this gives you the best leverage.

1 This is described right-handed; if you're a southpaw, reverse hands. Hold the mandrel horizontally in your left hand. Place the wire to be coiled over the top of the mandrel or the mandrel wire ①.

2 Grasp the wire with your right hand, about 2 to 3 inches (5.1 to 7.6 cm) away from the mandrel. Position the wire toward the end of the mandrel, on the right-hand side. Coil the wire over

the mandrel, then under and all the way around the mandrel 2. As the coil grows, the right hand moves away from the left hand, which is providing the leverage. As soon as you feel that happening, reposition the left hand closer to the right hand. To get a pristine coil, bring the piece of wire up and over to the left-hand side as you work, so it slides down the rightmost coil and right next to it 3.

3 If you started coiling at the middle of the wire, coil to approximately 1 inch (2.5 cm) from the end of the wire (this amount will work like a brake to keep the coil from spinning), then flip the mandrel over and coil the other half. You can trim off the wire sticking out on the ends, or work the

ends down around the mandrel using chain-nose pliers. When you find the right rhythm, you can get your coiling done in no time 4.

TIP You're looking to establish a rhythm. Lightly grasp the wire about 2 inches (5.1 cm) from where it first touches the mandrel and let it slide easily through your fingers.

4 When you run out of coiling wire or achieve the desired length, remove the coil from the mandrel.

TIPS
● Always coil away from your body; this ensures you'll use not only your hand, but your whole arm and shoulder.
● As you pull the wire around, head toward the rightmost coil and down to keep the coiling tight.
● If you have trouble holding the mandrel and wire, after you've coiled 1 inch (2.5 cm), use a ring clamp to hold the coil on the mandrel. This will take the pressure off your hand 5.

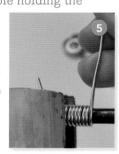

Jump rings

MAKING JUMP RINGS
The ability to make a jump ring of any size and gauge is a very important skill to have as a wire worker. It means you don't have to settle for the jump rings for sale in stores. Jump rings can be made in any diameter and from any gauge of wire. It's important to select an appropriate ring size and wire thickness, one that not only balances your piece of jewelry visually, but also that won't twist apart. Sometimes using two jump rings next to one another will make the piece stronger.

You can either coil on a mandrel, as was described under Hand Coiling, or you can coil on pliers.

COILING ON PLIERS

YOU'LL NEED
Wire, any gauge
Permanent marker
Round-nose pliers

1 Using a permanent marker, make a line at the place on your pliers around which you wish to make your jump rings. This will help you make each rotation at the same spot.

2 Next, grasp the end of your wire in between the pliers at the spot where you made the mark. The end of the wire should face vertically and it should not stick up above the tool 6.

3 Use the thumb from your other hand to push the wire tightly against the pliers as you rotate the tool away from you, approximately a third to a half turn. Loosen your grip on the tool and rotate it back to its starting position; then grasp the wire and rotate the pliers again in the same direction, once more using your thumb to push the wire up against the tool.

4 As the wire begins to pass itself, make sure the new wire goes between the end of the wire and the jaws of the tool; in other words, the end of the wire should move toward the tip of the pliers **7**. This way you'll achieve a coil rather than a cone.

TIP If you stay on the mark you drew on your pliers, you'll end up with jump rings that are the same size.

5 Continue coiling the wire around the pliers as described, until you have the length you desire **8**.

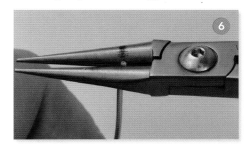

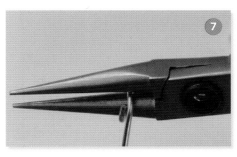

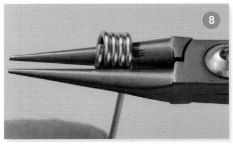

CUTTING COILS WITH FLUSH WIRE CUTTERS

Now that you have your coils, you need to cut them! There are a couple of choices: You can use a flush wire cutter or a jeweler's saw.

If you opt for flush wire cutters, first make sure that your cutters are capable of cutting the gauge of wire you're using. They also need to be sharp enough at the tips to make a smooth cut.

YOU'LL NEED
Coiled wire
Flush wire cutters

1 Examine the end of the coil and plan to make your first cut at the beginning of a full coil **9**. With the flush or flat side of the cutter toward the coil, trim off the end of the wire **10**. The end of the wire should be smooth **11**; if it's not, the tool was facing in the wrong direction. To correct this, flip the tool around and cut again, close to the original cut.

2 Next, flip the cutter over, line up the cutting edge of the tool with the cut end of the wire **12**, and clip off the first jump ring.

3 You'll notice a point on the end of the coil after you cut off the jump ring **13**. Flip the cutter over and trim this end off before cutting the next jump ring off the coil. So remember, for each jump ring you should trim, flip, and cut. Always remember to make two cuts per jump ring. If you were to cut straight through instead, you'd end up with one end flush cut and the other end with a point on it.

TIPS
● Control the tip of your cutters! Don't knick the coiled wire just beyond where you're cutting.
● The ends of the jump rings shouldn't be angled; make sure that the tips of the cutter are at 90° to the spot you're cutting.

CUTTING WITH A JEWELER'S SAW

To achieve the best and cleanest cuts, use a jeweler's saw with a 0/3 blade, which is small and makes a nice, clean cut.

YOU'LL NEED

Coiled wire

Jeweler's saw and 3/0 blade

Blade conditioner

Masking tape

Ring clamp

1 Apply a piece of masking tape on the side opposite where you'll saw, to keep the coil steadier and prevent the jump rings from dropping as you cut them. Rub some blade conditioner along the length of the coil in a section ¼ inch (6 mm) wide. (This product helps to keep the blade moving smoothly while you saw.)

2 Hold the coil in one hand, pinching at the base of the coils where you will cut. With the saw at an angle to the coil **14**, make a couple of downward strokes, creating a groove in the first few coils. This groove will act as a guide for the blade so it won't slide across the coil **15**. Saw one jump ring off at a time **16**.

TIP The secret to sawing is a loose grip on the handle and a fluid wrist. If you use a "death grip" you won't be able to cut and you may break the blade.

3 It gets hard to hold the coil when it gets really short. When you get down to the last four or five coils, run the saw across them all to cut them all at the same time.

TIP When you first start to saw, don't try to cut the whole coil at once. You run the risk of slipping and scratching all of the rings, so take your time.

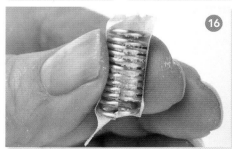

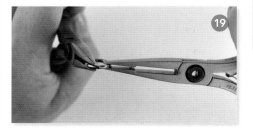

INSTALLING A BLADE IN A SAW FRAME

1 Loosen the nuts on both ends of the saw. Insert the blade in the jaws with the teeth facing out as well as down toward the handle.

2 Slide the blade in one of the ends and secure it by screwing the nut tight **20**.

3 The blade should fit no more than halfway inside the other end **21**, so adjust the length of the jaw as needed. Insert the blade, push the end of the saw frame up against the side of a table, and screw down the nut at the same time. The blade should be held tight enough that when you pluck it with your fingernail, it makes a pinging sound. If it sounds loose, try again.

OPENING AND CLOSING JUMP RINGS

When opening and closing jump rings you need to use two pliers with flat surfaces on the inside, meaning chain-nose, flat-nose, or bent-nose pliers 17. With a tool in each hand, and with each tool holding one end of the jump ring, twist one end toward you and the other end away 18. Opening it this way keeps the shape of the ring from distorting. Don't open the ring any wider than you need to, to make it easier to close.

When closing the ring, twist the ends so they line up then go past each other, and then work back and forth until you feel the ends grind together and line up 19. It's very important to close each ring carefully. If not, your jewelry may fall apart or feel rough in those spots.

FORGING

Forging uses a hammer to change the mass of metal to give it a different dimension and facets. Because it also compresses the molecules, it work-hardens the metal, which makes it stronger. Forging is interchangeably referred to as hammering throughout this book.

When hammering wire, each gauge requires the right amount of strength behind the hammer. If you strike too hard, you'll flatten out the wire too much, which looks unattractive. You'll also cause metal fatigue, and the wire could become brittle and break.

TIP Without a specific project in mind, forge the ends of some different gauges of wire to find out how much is too much. When does the metal become brittle? Knowing how far you can work the wire will tell you what you can do with it.

Hammering with the slightly domed flat side of the chasing hammer, the face, will leave a smooth, clean finish. The peen side will leave a distressed, textured look, rustic and lovely at the same time.

Each gauge of wire requires you to use a different level of force when hammering it. Smaller wire will need a gentle touch, while heavier wires call for a little more muscle.

After you've forged a piece of wire with the dome side to work-harden the wire 22, use the peen side to create texture 23.

Forged elements

FORGING PADDLES

Forging the end of the wire with a chasing hammer will spread it into a form like a paddle.

YOU'LL NEED

Wire*

Chasing hammer

Bench block and pad

Shown here with 2 inches (5.1 cm) of 14-gauge wire, but the length and gauge will vary depending on your purpose. This is also a good way to use scrap wire.

Paddles

SINGLE PADDLE

1 Flush-cut the end of the wire.

2 Place one end of the wire on the bench block and hold the other half so it is just off of the end of the block ㉔. Using the chasing hammer, strike the end of the wire many times and with a good amount of force. The goal is to spread the end of the metal into a paddle that is rounded on the edges. As you work, focus on the center of the chasing hammer and the very end of the wire ㉕.

3 Once the paddle is formed, travel up the wire with the hammer to *planish*, or smooth out, the roundness of the wire and to lengthen the look of the paddle.

4 Using an emery board, file and round off all flat or sharp edges.

DOUBLE-ENDED PADDLE

1 Flush-cut both ends of the wire

2 Hammer one end of the wire, forming a paddle as described in step 2 of Single Paddle.

3 Flip the piece over and, holding the first paddle in the forefinger and thumb, hold it on the same plane as the first side. Hammer the second side to form a paddle. Both of the paddles should lie on the same plane.

4 The whole piece of wire should not be flat, but should have a drawbridge effect. It should be flat at the paddles with a gradual rise at the center.

5 Using an emery board, file and round off all flat or sharp edges ㉖.

DOUBLE-ENDED PADDLE ON PERPENDICULAR PLANES

1 Flush-cut both ends of the wire

2 Hammer one end of the wire, forming a paddle as above.

3 Hold the first paddle with the forefinger and thumb so that the plane of the second paddle will lie at a 90° angle to the first one. Hammer the second side to form a paddle.

4 Using an emery board, file and round off all flat or sharp edges ㉗.

FORMING SPIRALS

While a coiled tube's identical loops all lie on separate planes, a spiral's loops—emanating from one central circle—lie on a single plane.

CLOSED SPIRAL

> **YOU'LL NEED**
>
> Wire, 16 to 14 gauge
> Round-nose pliers
> Chain-nose pliers
> Flush wire cutters

1 A spiral must start with a circle. However, it's in the nature of wire to form into a teardrop shape instead of a circle when it's wrapped around round-nose pliers. To counteract that tendency and form a circle instead, start by using round-nose pliers to crush the very end of the wire, creating a taper in the tip of the metal ㉘.

2 Then smooth the metal, using the round-nose pliers to make the wire conform to their shape. Finish the circle by pushing the wire against and around the pliers with your thumb ㉙.

3 Put the round-nose pliers down and pick up the chain-nose pliers. Grip the circle flat in the new tool. At the spot where the circle separates from the wire, push the wire against the circle to begin creating a spiral ㉚. Keep spiraling until you have two full revolutions ㉛.

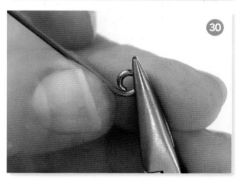

OPEN SPIRAL

YOU'LL NEED

Wire, 16 to 14 gauge
Round-nose pliers
Chain-nose pliers
Flush wire cutters

1 Use round-nose pliers to crush the very end of the wire, creating a taper in the tip of the metal. Then smooth the metal over the round-nose pliers, to make the wire conform to their shape. Finish the circle by pushing the wire against and around the pliers with your thumb **32**.

2 Put the round-nose pliers down and grip the circle flat in the chain-nose pliers. Hold the middle finger of the left hand under the wire that's coming out of the circle. With the right hand, push the wire against the finger while rotating the handle of the pliers up, counter-clockwise **33**. Repeat this process, taking baby steps **34**.

Both closed spirals and open spirals can be formed into head pins, as explained on page 19, but we'll open the discussion of head pins with simpler designs first.

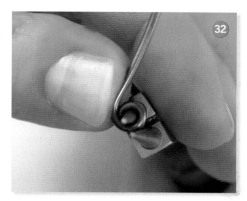

MAKING HEAD PINS

If you buy commercial head pins, you'll have to settle for what you can find. The advantage of making your own head pins is you can create them as long or as short as you like, in different styles and in any gauge. You can also control the size of the balls on the ends. (Ones that are larger or smaller than the few commercial options may be a better look for a given design.) Making all these adjustments will allow you to fit your beads perfectly—and even cap the tops if you like.

PADDLE HEAD PINS

Anyone can forge a paddled head pin. Just be careful not to make it too long; it could easily get caught on things.

YOU'LL NEED

Any gauge of wire

Flush wire cutters

Chasing hammer and block

1 Cut the wire to the desired length. Place one end of the wire on the block and strike it with the face of the hammer to cause the end to spread out ③⑤. Keep forging until the paddle shape is wide enough to not pass through the bead hole.

2 Finish up by filing the paddle shape to round the corners ③⑥.

BALLED HEAD PINS

This is a no-brainer skill with a real quick learning curve. You'll never buy another head pin after you see how easy this is to do!

To make the cleanest and most uniformly shaped balls, use fine silver wire. You can use sterling silver and copper, but they'll turn black and the balls will resemble a droplet. Sterling gets pitted, too, and anything heavier than 24-gauge copper will require a larger, hotter torch to get the metal to the melting point.

Balled head pins made from sterling silver (left) and fine silver (right).

YOU'LL NEED

Fine silver, 26 to 18 gauge

Flush wire cutters

Tweezers

Butane torch*

Fireproof surface**

Small bowl of water

Either a jewelry torch, or one from a kitchen store. Get one that self-ignites and has a stand.

**You can use a cookie sheet because its lip will catch any metal that drips off.*

1 Cut pieces of wire a little longer than you want your finished head pins to be.

2 Put the torch on the fireproof surface and ignite it. Most torches have a knob you can turn that allows you to make the flame fluffy or pointed. You want a pointed flame.

SAFETY FIRST!

Be certain to work on a fireproof surface, and have a small bowl of water on hand to quench the balled head pins after you make them. Make sure to work in a well-ventilated area. Crack a window if you don't have an exhaust fan. And safety glasses are always a good thing to wear.

3 Pick up the end of one of the cut wires with the tweezers. Coming from above, lower the tip of the wire into the pointed end of the blue flame.

- Thinner gauges will melt right away and the ball will run up the wire. You can keep the balls very small by removing them from the flame as the ball forms. If you want them bigger, continue to lower the wire into the flame. At a certain point the heat will be too much and the ball may fall off...it's lucky you're working on a fireproof surface! No worries; just start over. The head pin will just be shorter than you planned.

- For thicker wires, you'll need to "bathe" the wire in the flame, which means to slowly go up and down in the flame until the wire heats up enough to melt.

4 Drop the head pin into the water.

. . . .

TIP Make a lot of head pins ahead of time so you won't have to interrupt a project each time you need one. We like to make them of different gauges and lengths, so we're always prepared.

. . . .

SPIRAL HEAD PINS

Unlike balled head pins this fancy type has a spiral as the head.

1 Make a closed spiral (or an open spiral), working close to the tip of the pliers to make the initial circle as small as possible.

2 After making the two full revolutions, place the chain-nose pliers as far as possible into the angle formed by the wire exiting the spiral and the spiral itself. Hold the spiral with your left hand and give the pliers a quarter-turn to make a 90° angle just above the spiral **37**.

3 Using the face of the hammer, forge just the spiral, to strengthen it **38**, then texture it with the peen side of the hammer **39**.

. . . .

TIP Take care to hammer only the spiral; you want to retain elasticity in the straight part of the wire to complete the rest of the piece later.

. . . .

FINISHING VARIATIONS

After making a basic spiral head pin, you can do a number of cool things with it.

Open Spiral Loop

1 Make an open spiral head pin. Cut the remaining wire down to about ½ inch (1.3 cm).

The ear wires on Janice's Dog Bone Link Earrings started as a spiral head pin before she did additional shaping.

2 Grasp the end of the wire in the round-nose pliers and roll it in the direction opposite the spiral, until the

tip of the wire touches the top of the open spiral **40**. Forge the spirals, or not, as desired **41**.

Open Spiral with Perpendicular Loop

1 Make an open spiral head pin. Cut the remaining wire down to about ½ inch (1.3 cm).

2 Place the chain-nose pliers just above the second full revolution, grasping the wire. Give the pliers a quarter-turn to create a crisp 90° angle **42**.

3 Grasp the wire at the angle, and bend the wire toward you and perpendicular to the spiral **43**.

4 Grasp the end of the wire with the round-nose pliers and, rolling the pliers away from you, form a loop that sits perpendicular to the open spiral **44**.

Continued on next page.

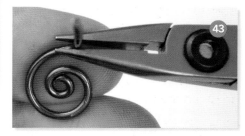

5 Forge, to strengthen  and texture .

Spiral Head Pin with Eye Loop

1 Make a spiral head pin and place a bead on it.

2 Next, you'll make a loop above the bead; start by placing the chain-nose pliers directly above the bead **47**. Turn your hand, taking care not to push against the bead too hard so it won't crack, and use your fingers to bend the wire at a crisp 90° angle. Grasping the end of the wire with round-nose pliers, roll the wire in to make a loop **48**. This loop doesn't need to be perfectly snug against the bead at this point because you're going to adjust it next **49**.

3 Visually estimate how much extra wire there is between the bead and the eye pin. Trim off that much wire **50**, then grasp the end of the wire with the round-nose pliers and roll the wire into the bead. The fit should be perfect **51**!

4 If desired, hammer the spiral to spread and texture the metal **52**.

MAKING EYE LOOPS

Eye loops can be used to connect one bead to another, or they can be linked to each other in a chain, with beads on them, or without.

1 Grip the end of the wire in the base of the round-nose pliers **53**. Bend the wire around the pliers, pushing the wire into the pliers to take on a round form **54**. Because you can't achieve a full loop in one movement, reposition your pliers and push the

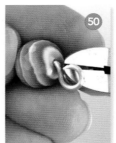

There's no standard name for these. Janice calls them "eye pins," Tracy says "eye loops," and still others simply use the name "loop." You'll probably come across all these terms during your adventures in wire beading, but in this book we'll call them eye loops.

wire the rest of the way around them to finish the circle (55).

2 Take the round-nose pliers out of the circle. Using the chain-nose pliers, grasp the portion of the wire inside the loop where the wires meet. Bend the wire back over the back of the pliers, until it looks like a duck's head (56).

3 Place the round-nose pliers back in the eye loop. With your thumb, reposition the eye so it's perpendicular to the pin. It should resemble a lollipop.

4 If desired, hammer the top of the eye loop. It looks nice either way (57).

. . . .

TIP You can vary the size of eye loops by shaping them at different spots along the pliers' jaw, as well as by changing the gauge of the wire. Use a gauge of wire that fills the bead hole.

. . . .

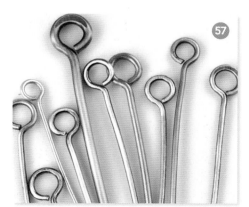

MAKING WRAPPED EYE LOOPS

This wrap will give you a bead held between wrapped sections of wire that end in loops. You can use this technique with wire or head pins.

YOU'LL NEED

A bead

Wire, or a head pin that fits through the bead's hole

Round-nose pliers

Chain-nose pliers

Flush wire cutters

Chasing hammer and block

SIDE ONE

1 Begin by marking the spot on your round-nose pliers around which you want to make your loop. (This way the loops on both sides of the bead will be the same size.) Place the wire vertically in the jaws, at the mark, with roughly 2 inches (5.1 cm) of wire sticking out the top (58).

2 Using your hand, push the wire at the top of the pliers away from you to create a right angle bend in the wire (59). Change your grip on the top of the bend, as shown in (60).

3 Grab the top end of the wire and roll it toward you down over the top of the pliers, until it points straight down (61). Rotate the pliers so the loop is on the bottom nose (62), then pull the wire around the tool to complete the loop. This loop should be loose enough that it rotates easily around the tip of the pliers. Transfer the tool to your other hand and position it with its tip pointing up. Grasp the end of the wrapping wire (this is the shorter end) with your chain-nose pliers (63), and wrap firmly around the bend once (64).

4 Wrap as many times as you like, depending on how much wire you have to work with. Two or three wraps look best. Trim the extra wrapping wire off with flush cutters (65). Finish by

placing the chain-nose pliers on the end of the wire. Squeeze, and rotate the tool in the direction of the coils. This will keep the end of the wire from sticking out and position it at the base of the coil. You have now completed the wrapped eye loop on one side.

SIDE TWO

5 Put the bead on the wire. Grip the wire with round-nose pliers against the free end of the bead, and hold the tool with the wire sticking straight up **66**. Use your hand to bend the wire away from you at a right angle. Check the angle. You want to have the same length of wire between the bend and the bead as you have for the wrap on the other side. If the lengths don't match up, straighten the wire and adjust the placement of the round-nose pliers.

6 Place the round-nose pliers at the top of the bend and repeat steps 3 and 4 on this side of the bead, as shown in **67** and **68**.

CREATING WRAPPED EYE LOOPS WITH SPIRAL CAPS

The wrapped portion forms a spiral cap that sits on the bead.

YOU'LL NEED

A bead
Balled head pin
Round-nose pliers
Chain-nose pliers
Flush wire cutters

1 Put the bead on the head pin. Where it exits from the bead, bend the end of the head pin at a right angle **69**. With the bead and ball of the pin facing you, and the wire pointing up, grasp the wire as shown in **70**.

2 Looking down at the nose of the plier, begin to rotate the plier away from you. Stop when you've made roughly half a loop **71**. Be careful not to go too far, or you'll pull out the 90° bend. Using your hand, pull the wire the rest of the way around to complete the loop **72**.

3 Place the tool in your other hand and wrap the wire around to close the loop **73**. Then spiral the wire over the top of the bead. Once you have as much spiraling as you desire, cut off the extra wire, making sure to make the cut parallel to, and lined up with, the side of the loop **74**. This gives a more finished look than cutting it off in a different place.

MAKING DOUBLE-LOOP EYE WRAPS WITH SPIRAL CAPS

YOU'LL NEED

A bead that allows 18-gauge wire to pass through

10 inches (25.4 cm) of 18-gauge wire

Flush wire cutters

Long round-nose pliers

Chain-nose pliers

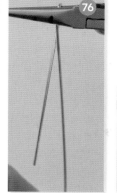

TIP On the round-nose pliers, use a permanent marker to indicate the spot where you want to make the loops. This way they'll all be the same size!

SIDE ONE

1 Grasp the wire in the round-nose pliers (on the mark you made), leaving approximately 2 inches (5.1 cm) of wire above the tool 75. Holding the wire from below in your fingers, rotate the pliers away from you, turning only as far as is comfortable 76. Loosen your grip on the wire, rotate the tool back to its original position, then rotate the tool away again to complete the shaping of the loop 77.

TIPS

● As you rotate, the end of the wire that sticks up above the tool must pass on the open side of the tip end of the pliers (rather than the side with the handle) or you won't be able to make both of the loops the same size.

● Always keep the wire below the tool oriented vertically.

2 Remove the loop from the pliers. Reposition the round-nose pliers with the marked nose furthest from you and place the loop back on the tool on the mark you made, as shown in 78. Rotate the pliers away from you to create a second loop, stopping when the short end of the wire points straight up 79. Remove the loops of wire from the tool.

3 Keeping the loops in the same position, grasp them with the chain-nose pliers and pull the wire to create an angle at the base of the loop 80.

TIP Don't be afraid to exaggerate this angle by pulling hard on the wire. This is referred to as "breaking the neck" and it creates a nice crisp angle under the loop.

4 Place the loop back on the round-nose pliers; hold the tool in your non-dominant hand with the tip pointing up 81. (If the working wire isn't pointing toward you, reposition the loop so that it is.) Grasp the working wire with your dominant hand and fold it over, away from you, keeping the wire tucked right in the bend and close to the loop 82. Don't cut off the extra wire.

SIDE TWO

5 Place the bead on the wire. Use the round-nose pliers to grasp the wire approximately 1½ inches (3.8 cm) from the bead—the amount may vary depending on how big the loops are (83). Holding the bead with your other hand, rotate the tool away from you, letting the end of the wire pass around the tip end of the pliers (84).

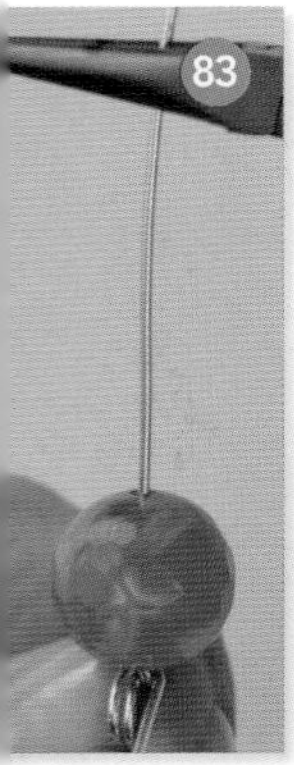

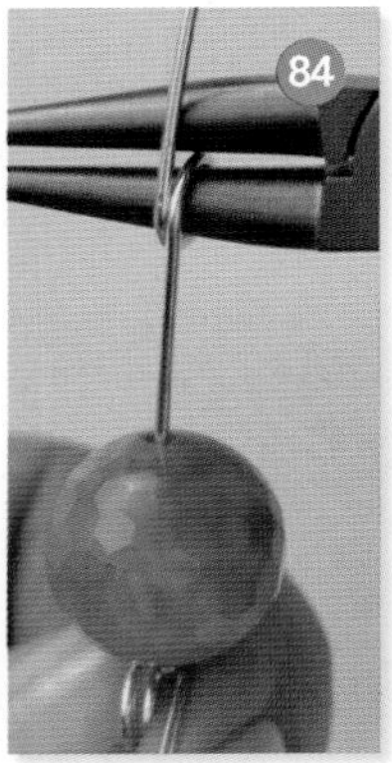

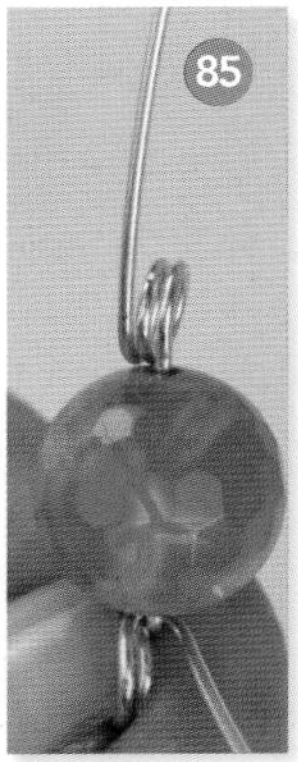

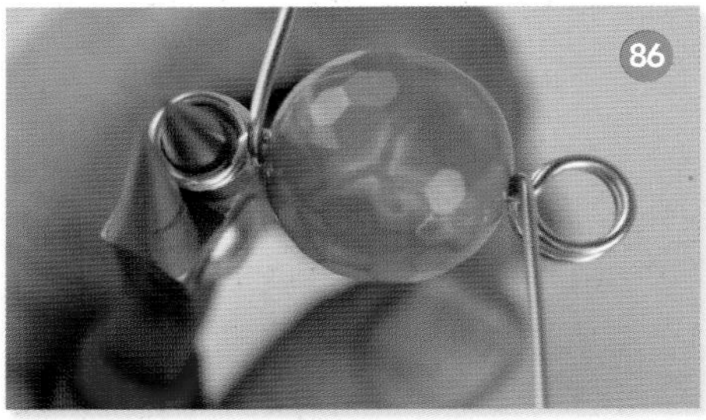

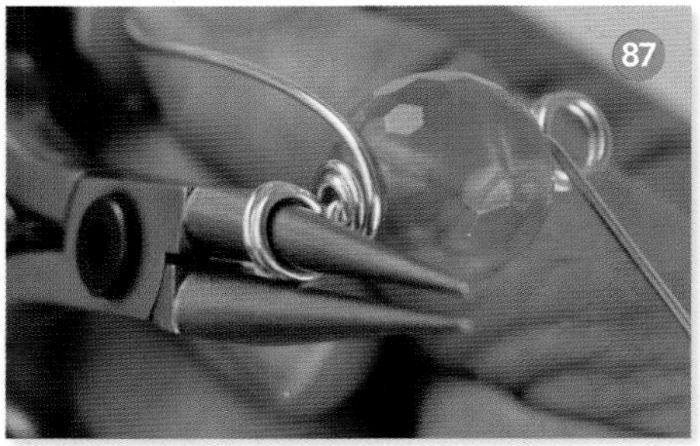

6 After one complete rotation, reposition the round-nose pliers onto the mark of the nose that's furthest from you, then rotate the tool again until you've formed a second complete loop. The end of the wire should stick straight up and the loops should be right against the bead (85) (see Tip below).

7 With the chain-nose pliers in the loops, pull the tool toward you to bend an angle in the wire under the loop and on top of the bead. Place the loops on the round-nose pliers and hold the tool in your non-dominant hand, with the nose of the pliers pointing up. Fold the wire over to secure the loops (86).

8 Leaving the loops on the round-nose pliers, grab the end of the wire with your hand or chain-nose pliers and spiral the wire several times over the end of the bead, capping it (87). Also form a spiral cap on side one, as well, then cut off the extra wire from both sides, making sure to line up the cut parallel to and lined up with the loops.

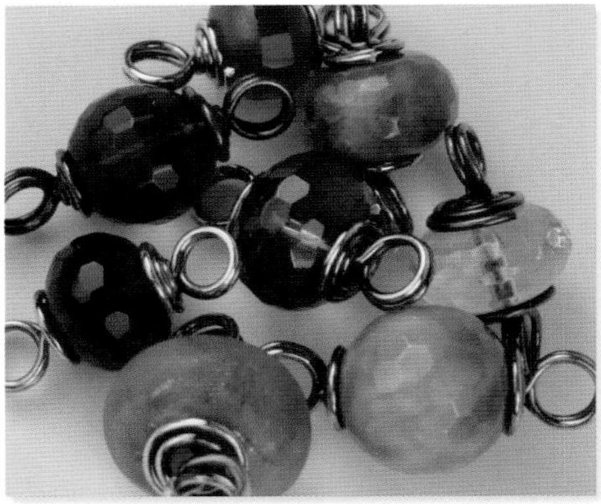

Wrapped eye loops with spiral caps have a nice, substantial look.

CLASPS

A hand-made closure will match your jewelry better than a commercial clasp. Here, we offer you a few different styles.

HOOK CLASPS

YOU'LL NEED

- 4 inches (10.2 cm) of 14-gauge wire
- Flush wire cutters
- Chasing hammer
- Bench block and pad
- Round-nose pliers
- Multibarrel pliers

TIP If the two complete loops you've made aren't against the bead (88), reinsert the round-nose pliers into the loops using the nose furthest away from you (89). Make a turn away from yourself, loosen your grip, and rotate the pliers back to the original position (90). Pull the wire back to the straight-up position (91). Repeat, until the loop is on top of the bead (92).

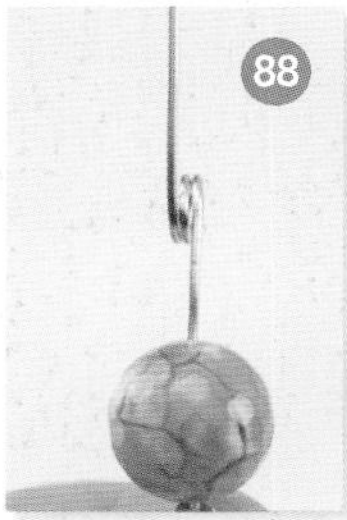

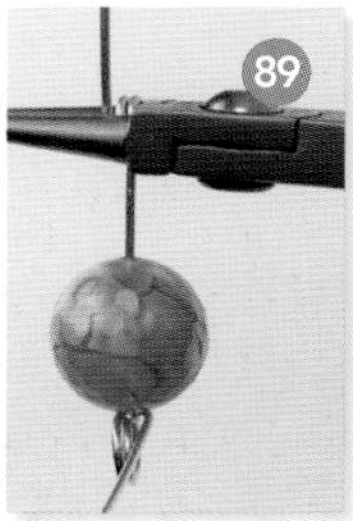

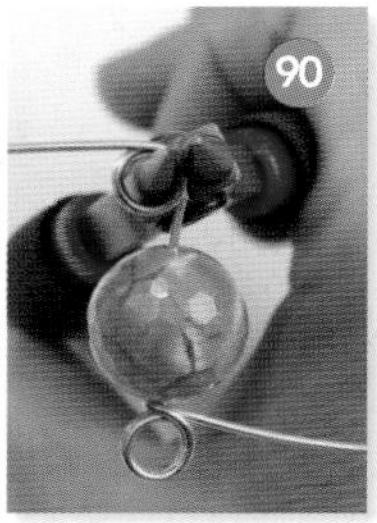

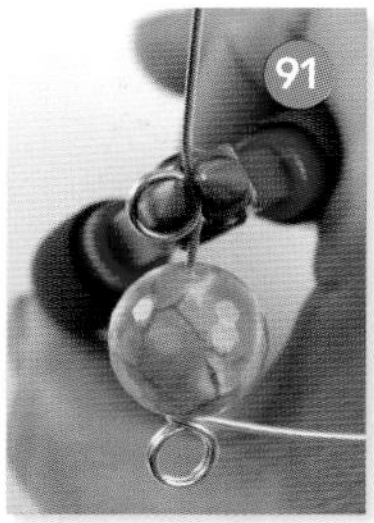

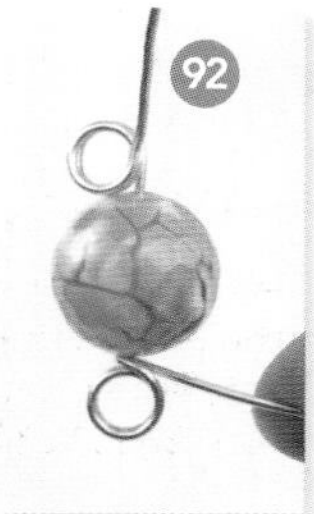

1 Trim the ends of the wire flush. Place it on the bench block and flatten approximately ¾ inch (1.9 cm) of both ends with the chasing hammer until each is as thin as paper. The wire should be tapered in thickness (93).

TIP If the end of the wire starts to curve as you're flattening it, flip it over and strike from the other side.

2 File the flattened wire to make smooth corners.

3 Grasp one end of the wire in the round-nose pliers, as close to the tip as possible. Roll the tool away from you, creating a loop. Make another hand rotation so the loop overlaps itself by a half-turn.

TIP It's best to use small round-nose pliers, to make the loop as little as possible.

4 The loop on the other end needs to face the same way as the first. For this side, grasp the flattened end in the round-nose pliers three-quarters of the way up the nose of the tool, which will create a larger loop. Rotate the tool to create a loop that's a revolution and a half **94**.

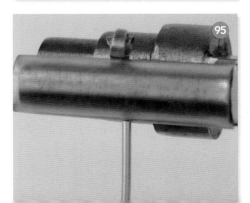

5 Grasp the smaller of the loops in the multibarrel pliers, with the loop facing you **95**. Roll the tool away from you to create the hook **96**.

· ·

TIP You can make adjustments to the clasp by placing it on a different portion of the multibarrel pliers to make it larger or smaller. For example, if the hook is too large, you can make it smaller by rotating the larger loop side more to take up some of the wire.

· ·

6 Use your chasing hammer to forge or flatten the top of the curve **97**.

A trio of hook clasps; as shown in the one at the right, if the clasp hook is large enough, you can flatten two sections on either side of the top of the hook.

HOOK CLASP WITH A WRAPPED LOOP

YOU'LL NEED

Wire, 16 to 14 gauge
Flush wire cutters
Round-nose pliers
Chain-nose pliers
Multibarrel pliers
Chasing hammer
Bench block and pad

1 Cut 5 inches (12.7 cm) of wire. *Note:* this can be longer or shorter depending on whether you want to make a larger or smaller clasp.

2 Make a wrapped eye loop (described in steps 1 through 4 on page 21) on one end of the wire. When making this loop, start with approximately 2 inches (5.1 cm) of wire above the round-nose pliers. After making it, finish off the rest of the wire by coiling it under the loop and cutting off the excess **98**.

3 Using the flat-nose pliers, make a 45° angle in the wire, just above the coil **99**.

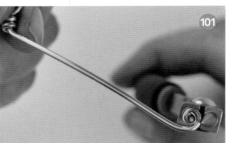

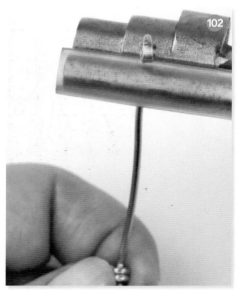

4 Forge approximately ½ inch (1.3 cm) at the end of the wire so it tapers to paper-thin 100 .

5 Make a small loop on the forged end, using the tip of small round-nose pliers. This loop needs to be turned toward the bottom wrapped loop 101 . Place this end in the multi-barrel pliers with the loop facing you 102 , then roll the plier away from you to create a hook.

· ·

TIP If you don't own multibarrel pliers, you can shape the end of the clasp around a dowel or even a marker—anything that's the appropriate size.

· ·

6 Use the chasing hammer to flatten both the top of the curve and the loop, as shown in 103 and 104 .

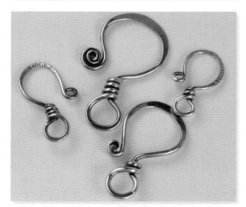

You can vary the look of a hooked clasp with a wrapped loop by making the hook rounder, or narrow and tall.

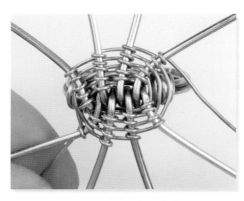

BASKET WEAVING

Basket weaving with wire emulates traditional basketry making and can take on many forms. Basically, basket weaving is comprised of two gauges of wire, one as the warp wire and one as the weft. Warp wires are heavier and stronger, so they're used for the armature, and weft wires are woven in and around the warp wires. There are many ways to basketweave; we'll go into more detail in each project.

A FEW NON-WIRE TECHNIQUES

USING RING MANDRELS

After a ring is finished, if you discover it's a bit too small, you can increase its size. You'll need to use a metal mandrel. (The wooden mandrel will simply not provide the support you need when hammering.) Place the shank of the ring on the mandrel and hammer it gently to spread the wire of the shank, thereby increasing the size of the ring.

REAMING BEADS

When making a hole just a little bit bigger, we use the hand reamer. Dip the reamer in some water and move the tip in and out of the hole to file out a little material **105**. (Putting water on the bit limits the dust, keeps the bead cooler, and lengthens the life of the reamer bit.) If you need to make the hole much larger, you may want to use the electric reamer; it will take much less time. Don't forget to wet it! When you're finished, make sure to dry off the bit so it doesn't rust.

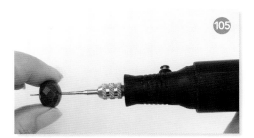

FINISHING

Some people are what we call "Shiny Girls." They're not interested in antiquing their pieces. While that's not how we roll, it's perfectly okay. There's not much to explain for them, though. Remove any permanent marker left on the wire with an alcohol pad. Then shine up the jewelry with a polishing cloth for a brilliant finish.

But for information on adding a nice, warm patina, read on.

. . . .

ANTIQUING

After making your pieces, you may decide to give them a *patina*, a burnished sheen that makes a piece look aged and that gives a piece more visual depth. Liver of sulfur is used to patina, or "antique," sterling silver, fine silver, copper, and bronze. It won't react with gold, gold-filled, brass, or pewter.

Liver of sulfur smells like rotten eggs. It is, after all, sulfur! It comes in a solid, a liquid, or a gel. You can use any of these forms.

Heat up your liver of sulfur solution in a small crockpot (one reserved *only* for this process) and keep it hot during use. (*Never* boil liver of sulfur as that releases toxic fumes.) The hotter the piece and the hotter the solution, the faster it works, but it also gives off a stronger smell.

SAFETY FIRST!

You should mix up your solution in either a glass or a plastic container. Wear plastic gloves and work in a well-ventilated area. Liver of sulfur is toxic, so do not use tools or containers that have held this chemical for food preparation; that includes your microwave oven.

CLOCKWISE FROM TOP, liquid and gel-form liver of sulfur, steel wool, liver of sulfur in dry form, tweezers resting on a solution of liver of sulfur

There's nothing wrong with using the solution cold. It just takes a bit longer to work. Instead of seconds to antique, it may take a minute for copper and up to four minutes for silver.

A different method some people prefer is to heat up the jewelry or components in hot water and then drop them into the cold liver of sulfur. With this approach, they achieve a quick reaction without having to heat the liver of sulfur, and it keeps the smell to a minimum.

USING LIVER OF SULFUR

YOU'LL NEED

Liver of sulfur in solid, liquid, or gel form

A dedicated glass or plastic container with a lid

Plastic fork or tweezers

Water

1 Read all the instructions before you start. Place a pea-sized piece of liver of sulfur—or half a teaspoon (5 ml) of the liquid or gel—in the container. Run your tap water until it's as hot as it gets. Pour ½ to 1 cup (118.3 to 236.6 ml) of tap water over the liver of sulfur to dissolve it.

2 Place your piece in the solution . It will oxidize in stages—first a gold color, then peacock shades, finally to gray and, ultimately, black. You'll want to take it out when it's gray. It doesn't need to go all the way black.

3 Retrieve your piece from the solution with a plastic fork or tweezers , or use a small task basket for tiny parts. Avoid immersing your hands in the solution. Rinse the piece thoroughly with tap water.

When you're finished with the liver of sulfur solution, place a lid on the container. The next time you need to antique, check the solution. If it's still yellow, it's still usable. Antique away! Depending on weather conditions (hot or cold), the strength of the solution, and the freshness of the liver of sulfur, it can last from a day to weeks before it no longer works.

To dispose of liver of sulfur permanently, put it away under your sink, in your garage, or outside for a few days. Its color will change from yellow to foggy to clear, at which point it's neutralized and harmless, and you can throw it away outside or pour it down the sink. To neutralize it immediately, sprinkle in a small amount of baking soda then wash it down the drain with running water.

ANTIQUING BRASS

Brass looks absolutely gorgeous with a patina. You'll need to use a different solution to antique it. There are different products on the market, described as various things (for example brass ager and brass aging solution), but they all have the same chemical ingredients: phosporic acid and selenium.

SAFETY FIRST!

Be extra cautious when using these products. Read all of the directions and warnings on the bottle before using. Work in a well-ventilated room and wear rubber gloves; contact with the skin can sting, and besides, cleanup is very messy.

YOU'LL NEED

Fine steel wool

Solution for antiquing brass

Plastic container

Tweezers

Water

1 Scrub your finished wire piece with the steel wool to remove any anti-tarnish coating that may be on the wire.

2 Pour the solution into the plastic container. Place your piece into it and wait for it to turn black. This may take seconds, or up to a minute.

3 Remove the piece from the solution using tweezers, and rinse it off with water. Wipe it with a paper towel; this removes some of the black finish.

4 Use steel wool or a polishing pad to highlight and set the finish.

The solution is re-usable, so there's no need to dispose of it. You can pour the solution back in the bottle, or store it in a leak-proof container with a snap-on lid. If you wish to dispose of the antiquing solution, check the manufacturer's instructions for the proper way to do so.

POLISHING

Gently buff off any patina with 4/0 (also sold as 0000) fine steel wool or a polishing pad. This will remove the patina from raised surface areas, but not recessed ones **3**. Take your time here. This is the part that no one enjoys, but it must be done.

Give the piece a final polish using a polishing cloth, or place it in a tumbler.

Tumbler

TUMBLING

YOU'LL NEED

A medium-sized rock tumbler

2 pounds (907 g) of combination stainless steel shot*

Burnishing compound**

A sink

*This consists of different shapes and sizes

**You can use dish soap instead, as long as it does not contain any extra additives such as anti-bacterial agents, which will adversely affect the shot and the tumbler barrel.

1 Place the shot in the tumbler, then add your jewelry. Add a capful of burnishing compound or a small squirt of dish soap. Fill the tumbler with water 1 inch (2.5 cm) above the jewelry. The tumbler shouldn't be more than two-thirds full. Secure the lid.

2 Depending on the piece, tumble from 30 minutes to an hour. If the piece is small, with few nooks and crannies, it will only require 30 minutes. If it's a three-dimensional piece, leave it in for longer.

3 After you finish tumbling, pour the shot and tumbled pieces in a strainer and rinse well. Allow the shot to dry before putting it away.

TIPS

● Some beads can be damaged by tumbling. Be aware of what you're putting in the machine. If you're not familiar with how a bead will react in the tumbler, it's best to do a test run. Put an extra bead in the tumbler first, and see how it comes out. Doing this can save you a lot of heartache!

● Most pearls will be okay, but some might lose their color or finish, so test one.

● Hard semiprecious stones will do fine in a tumbler. Soft stones, such as turquoise, should not be tumbled.

● All glass, including crystals, will be fine—unless it has a special applied finish, such as AB.

● Anything organic—including bone, pods, shell, coral, and spiny oyster—is porous and should not be put in the tumbler.

● The most important thing to keep in mind when using a tumbler: if you would just die if something happened to the piece you tumbled, don't put it in the tumbler—hand polish it!

DOG BONE EARRINGS

by Janice Berkebile   Dangle a pair of your favorite beads from a paddle link. People will be mesmerized by the glint of light reflecting from these simple, pretty earrings.

. . . .

Tip: When you're creating two (or more) of anything that you want to look identical, make the items at the same time, then proceed to the next step. In other words, don't build one earring, then the other. Instead, make them in tandem.

. . . .

DOG BONE LINK

Make one for each earring.

1 Use the large-gauge flush wire cutters to cut a piece of 12-gauge wire 1 inch (2.5 cm) long, with both ends trimmed flush.

2 Place one end of the wire on the bench block and hold the other half so it hangs just off of the end of the block **1**. Using the chasing hammer, spread the very end of the metal into a paddle with rounded edges **2**. This will take many strikes of the hammer. As you work, focus the center of the chasing hammer on the very end of the wire. Once the paddle is formed, travel up the wire with the hammer to smooth it out and to lengthen it.

3 Forge a paddle on the other end of the wire so that it lies on the same plane as the first paddle. The piece of wire should have a flat bottom, with thin paddles that rise gradually to meet at the center.

4 Using an emery board, sand and round off all the edges **3**.

5 Mark where you want to punch the holes **4**, being sure to center them in the paddles. Punch the holes **5**. If the hole punch leaves a burr, place the dog bone link back on the block and tap the burr gently with the chasing hammer to remove it.

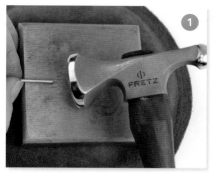

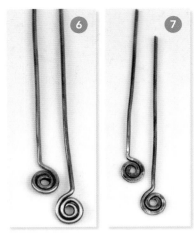

SPIRAL EAR WIRES

Make one for each earring.

6 Cut a piece of 18-gauge wire 2⅝ inches (6.7 cm) long. Spiral one end two full revolutions. Create a 90° angle at the end of the spiral **6**.

7 Place both spirals on the bench block so they face in opposite directions. Hammer them one at a time to flatten them, then flip the hammer over and texture them **7**.

8 Holding the wire in your hand, place the tip of the pliers just beyond the

spiral **8**. Roll the tool away to create a small loop from which the dog bone links will hang **9**.

9 Using the base of the long round-nose pliers, grasp the wire ⅛ inch (3 mm) above the spiral **10**. Roll the wire into the plier until it touches the other side

of the wire 11, creating the curve in the ear wire. Hammer the top of the ear wire to work-harden it. Make a small bend at the tail end of the wire with the chain nose pliers 12. File the tail end of the ear wire with an emery board 13.

ASSEMBLE

10 On a head pin, place a 9-mm spacer, a lampwork bead, and then a 6-mm spacer. Begin a wrapped eye loop but, before you complete the wrap, slide the headpin through one of the holes in the dog bone link. Finish the wrap and trim the end of the wire 14.

. . . .

Tip: Wire-wrapped glass beads should always have metal spacers next to them, on both sides. This protects the fragile glass.

. . . .

11 Slide the hole at the other end of the dog bone link onto one of the earwires. Slide it past the large curve and into the small curve.

12 To assemble the other earring, repeat steps 10 and 11.

VARIATION

DOG BONE BRACELET

by Janice Berkebile

Get your sparkle on wearing this bracelet! Combine wrapped dog bone links with vintage crystals to bring on the bling.

YOU'LL NEED

4 inches (10.2 cm) of 12-gauge dead-soft copper

20 inches (50.8 cm) of 20-gauge dead-soft silver wire

3 inches (7.6 cm) of 16-gauge dead-soft silver wire

4 green vintage crystals, 7 mm

One 14-gauge sterling silver jump ring, 6 mm

One 14-gauge sterling silver jump ring, 4 mm

Liver of sulfur

Ruler

Large-gauge flush wire cutter

Chasing hammer

Bench block and pad

Hole punch for metal, 1.8 mm

Round-nose pliers

Chain-nose pliers

Long round-nose pliers

DOG BONE LINKS

1 Cut five pieces of 12-gauge wire, each ⅝ inch (1.6 cm) long, and flush-cut both ends of each piece. Referring to page 31, forge these into double-ended paddles. File the ends of each link so they're rounded .

. . . .

Tip: When cutting multiple pieces of wire of the same length, measure one piece against the ruler, and match the rest to the first piece you cut.

. . . .

2 Punch a hole in each end of every link ❷. To do so, place the hole punch on the end where you desire the hole. Double- and triple-check the placement to ensure the tool isn't near the edge of the metal. Squeeze the punch, hold on to the metal, and wiggle the tool to get the link off of it.

3 Place the 20-gauge wire over the center of one link, with about ⅜ inch (1 cm) of wire facing toward you. Wrap it twice around the link, as tightly as possible, then cut the long end to ⅜ inch (1 cm) ❸. Form a spiral seated on the same side of the link in both ends of the wire ❹. Repeat, using the remaining wire to wrap the other four links in the same way.

ANTIQUE

Oxidize the links, the remaining 20-gauge wire, and the as-yet unused 16-gauge wire. Clean up the links.

ASSEMBLE THE LINKS

The links are connected with wrapped eye loops that each have one crystal on them. As you assemble the chain, make sure the links all face the same direction.

4 Using the 20-gauge wire, start making a wrapped eye loop, remembering to slide on a paddle link before you wrap ❺. Trim off any extra wire. Slide on a crystal ❻.

5 Bend the wire at 90° directly out of the hole of the bead, taking care not to chip the crystal. Make a wrapped eye loop on this end, remembering to connect another paddle link to it before closing it **7**. Continue in this fashion until you've connected all five dog bone links into a chain.

Tip: If you discover the links aren't all facing the same direction, don't cut the chain apart; simply twist the two eye loops on each side of the problem link so it faces the right way.

CLASP

Using the 16-gauge wire, make a hook clasp with a wrapped loop. (Form the hook portion of the clasp around the base of the long round-nose pliers.) Forge the top portion of the clasp as well as the initial loop **8**.

FINISH

6 Connect the clasp to one end of the chain, using the 4-mm jump ring.

7 Attach the 6-mm jump ring to the other end of the chain. The clasp latches into this ring to close the bracelet.

GO-TO BRACELET by Tracy Stanley

I call this "go-to" because it's a great basic style that looks totally different depending on the type of beads you include. It might be your everyday bracelet or, gussied up with crystals or pearls instead of stone beads, something fancy for a night on the town.

YOU'LL NEED

60 inches (1.5 m) of 18-gauge dead-soft sterling silver wire

3 feet (91.4 cm) of 14-gauge dead-soft sterling silver wire

5 or 6 round or rondelle beads, 12 to 14 mm

1 accent bead, 8 to 10 mm

1 spacer, 4 to 6 mm

1 balled head pin

Liver of sulfur

Long round-nose pliers

Chain-nose pliers

Flat-nose pliers

Large-gauge flush wire cutters

Chasing hammer

Bench block and pad

Multibarrel pliers (optional)

Texturing hammer (optional)

Tip: Although the bracelet is shown here in silver, it looks just as good made of copper wire.

WIRE-WRAPPED BEADS

Cut the 18-gauge wire into six 10-inch (25.4 cm) pieces. Using the double-loop eye wrap with spiral cap technique, wire-wrap each of the round or rondelle beads .

Tip: If you want to use beads that have holes too small to accommodate your wire, use a bead reamer to make the holes larger, or switch to a smaller gauge of wire.

JUMP RINGS

Using between 18 and 24 inches (45.7 and 61 cm) of 14-gauge wire, make 14 to 16 jump rings at the bottom of your round-nose pliers. Make one ring slightly larger than the others—it will serve as the catch for the clasp to latch into later.

ACCENT BEAD

Slide the spacer on the head pin, add the accent bead, and finish off the wire by making a wrapped eye loop with spiral cap .

SPIRAL DANGLE

Cut 4 inches (10.2 cm) of the 14-gauge wire and make an open spiral with a perpendicular loop on top. Forge the spiral area with the chasing hammer .

Tip: The dangle is a great opportunity to use a texturing hammer to create a unique look.

CLASP

Cut 4 inches (10.2 cm) of 14-gauge wire and make a hook clasp **4**.

FINISH

Antique and polish all of the components **5**.

ASSEMBLE

1 Open all the jump rings. Make a chain by connecting the wire-wrapped beads, with two side-by-side jump rings. **6** shows the first two elements linked together.

Tip: The number of beads and jump rings you'll need will vary depending on the size and shape of the beads. You can add extra jump rings on the ends if adding another bead would make the bracelet too large. If you're uncertain of sizing, just add extra jump rings to the end without the clasp, creating an extension chain; you can catch the clasp into any of these rings for a proper fit.

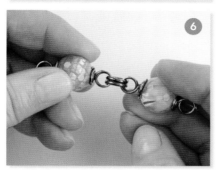

2 Attach the clasp to one end of the chain using a jump ring ❼. On the other end, link as many jump rings as necessary to achieve the desired length of the finished bracelet. Finally, attach the largest jump ring at the very end to serve as the catch for the clasp ❽.

3 Use a single jump ring to attach the accent bead and the loop of the spiral dangle to the larger spiraled end of the clasp ❾.

Tip: Adding charms, dangles, and accent beads near the ends of the bracelet will add weight and prevent the clasp from rotating to the top of your wrist during wear.

Now that you've completed this bracelet, why not make yourself a matching necklace?

CHAIN AND BEAD EARRINGS

by Tracy Stanley

These earrings make an outfit extra special, but they're also perfect for wearing every day. Make them short or make them long—it's your call. One thing's for sure: you'll love the attention you get when you wear them!

YOU'LL NEED

1 foot (30.5 cm) of 24-gauge dead-soft sterling silver wire

Piece of chain, 6 links long*

2 beads, 8 mm

28 beads, 4 to 6 mm**

Twenty-six 24-gauge balled head pins

2 ear wires

Small round-nose pliers

Chain-nose pliers

Flush wire cutters

*See the tip box below

**See the tip box at top right

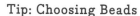

Tip: Choosing Chain

You can find chain in all different styles and materials. For this project, I prefer a chain that comes in a bar-and-loop style. If you can't find chain like this, you can use any linked chain; just get more than six links, and leave some links empty between the beads you add starting at step 4.

Tip: Choosing Beads

Select beads that not only look good together because of their color, but also beads of different shapes and types. Mixing it up will make for a more interesting look, so go for faceted, transparent, opaque, round, and bicone. You'll need two of each bead type so that your earrings match.

1 Cut the chain in half so you have two identical sections containing the same amount of links. Set one piece aside, to make the second earring later.

Tip: It's easiest to antique the chain, wire, and head pins before you start making your earrings. The chain is much easier to clean up without anything attached to it.

2 Using small round-nose pliers, make a wrapped eye loop at one end of the wire. Put on an 8-mm bead ①.

3 Make a wrapped eye loop on the other end, but before closing it, slide on a section of chain ②. Finish the loop, trim off any extra wire, and set it aside to use to make the second earring later.

4 You're going to work from the top of the earring down. Choose six beads for the topmost cluster. (Make sure to set aside the matching six beads to make the second earring later.) Place each bead onto a head pin and make a loop on each, but don't close the loops ③.

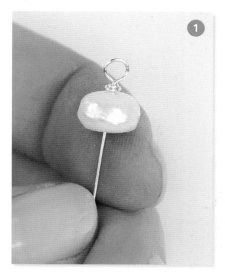

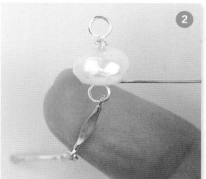

Tip: I usually pick the smaller beads in a combination that will look balanced from side to side.

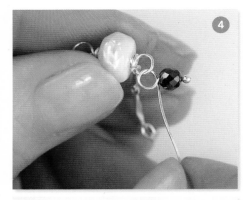

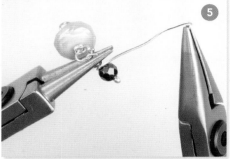

5 Slide one of these beads onto the loop at the base of the bead that has the chain on it **4**. Wrap the loop closed **5** and cut off any extra wire **6**.

6 Repeat step 5 to attach the other five beads, so that you have three on each side of the chain **7**.

7 Select three beads for the next cluster. (As done previously, set aside three matching beads to make the second earring later.) As described in step 4, string them on head pins and make loops. Attach them to the next available link that's between the chain bar, with two on one side of the chain and one on the other side **8**.

8 For the next section, select three beads, and as done previously, set aside three matching ones to make the second earring later. As described in step 4, put them onto head pins and make loops. Attach them to the next available link along the chain, hanging one on the side where you'd previously hung two, and two on the side where you previously hung one **9**.

9 Place two beads (set the matches aside) on one balled head pin and make a loop. Attach this to the bottom of the chain **10**.

10 Attach an ear wire **11**.

11 Repeat steps 2 through 10 to make the second earring.

Now that you've made one pair, experiment: These earrings can be made longer or shorter, with multiple chains or more clusters of beads. Let your imagination be your guide, and have fun!

CHAIN AND BEAD NECKLACE

by Tracy Stanley

This fun necklace can be made choker length or long enough to wrap around your neck twice. The chain keeps it light and airy. If you really want to make a statement, make two or three in graduating sizes and wear them all at the same time!

YOU'LL NEED

6 feet (1.8 m) of 24-gauge dead-soft sterling silver wire*

6 feet (1.8 m) of 22-gauge dead-soft sterling silver wire*

4 inches (10.2 cm) of 14-gauge dead-soft sterling silver wire

15 inches (38.1 cm) of chain**

Beads***

14 spacers, 6 to 7 mm

12 spacers, 8 mm

Two 14-gauge sterling silver jump rings, 7 mm

18 to 20 silver balled head pins, 24 gauge

3 silver charms****

Flush wire cutters

Ruler

Small round-nose pliers

Chain-nose pliers

Flat-nose pliers

Chasing hammer

Bench block and pad

Multibarrel pliers

Exactly how much wire you need depends on the length you make your necklace, the size of the beads, and the hole sizes of the beads.

**The links should allow 22-gauge wire to pass through. The amount of chain to get may vary, depending on the final length of necklace you desire and on the size of the links. You'll be cutting out a link with each section; if they're large, you may need to get a little extra chain. Using different types of chain in the same necklace can make for a nice look. You can even add more than one chain to the same section for an interesting and heavier appearance.*

***See the tip box at top right*

****If the charms don't come with jump rings, also get one jump ring for each.*

Tip: The shape and type of beads to use is up to you. Just look for a nice mix: round, rondelle, coin, faceted or smooth, pearl, stone, glass, crystal, even shell. Exact size isn't important. Use the following list just as a rough guide.

● 1 silver bead, 8 mm, with a hole that allows 14-gauge wire to pass through

● 14 assorted beads, 10 to 11 mm

● 4 assorted beads, 12 mm

● 4 faceted rondelles, 15 to 16 mm

● 2 coin-shaped beads, 20 mm

● 18 to 20 assorted beads, 4 to 6 mm

BEAD THE CHAIN

1 Cut five pieces of chain, each 1½ inches (3.8 cm) long. Set aside the silver bead for making the clasp later. Arrange your 22 largest beads and the spacers any way you like, aiming for an even distribution and a nice balance. Some of the beads can be doubled up.

Tip: Use more or less chain depending on the desired length of your necklace.

2 Using either the 22-gauge or the 24-gauge wire—whichever fits through your first bead—make a loop, catch one end of one of the sections of chain in it 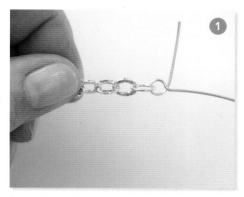, and wrap the loop closed 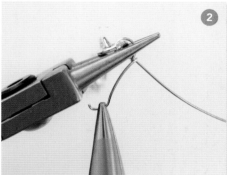.

3 Place your first bead (surrounded on each side by spacers, if desired) on the wire and capture it by finishing the wire off with a wrapped eye loop .

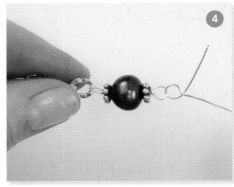

4 Make another loop and attach it to the already-made wrapped eye loop ④, then wrap it closed. As before, add a bead and spacers, then make a wrapped eye loop on the other end ⑤.

5 Repeat step 4 until you've attached a total of five or six beads in a row. Before you close the second loop in the fifth wrapped eye loop, catch a section of chain in it.

6 Continue adding beads, spacers where desired, and sections of chain until you have four connected sections of beads, with chain on both ends.

· ·

Tip: As long as the next component on the necklace is a wrapped eye loop with beads on it, you don't need to worry about adding anything to the second loop before you close it. When you want to add chain, however, you need to add it before you close the loop. Don't be surprised if you forget to do this every once in a while!

· ·
· ·

Tip: From time to time, hold up your work and make sure the beaded chain has a nice balance. Don't be afraid to change up your original design if you think it would look better. Consider not only the size but the type of bead when you're placing each on. It isn't nearly as interesting to have all one type or shape of bead consecutively, for example. Mix it up—have some fun!

· ·

7 You can alter the overall length by adding more or less chain at both ends of the beaded chain, in the area that will be worn at the back of the neck. Here's how: Add a wrapped eye loop with a single bead on it to one end of the beaded chain, catching whatever length of chain you desire for the back of the neck in the second loop you wrap. Attach a 7-mm jump ring to the end of the chain just added ⑥. Repeat on the other side of the beaded chain.

TO ANTIQUE OR NOT...
***THAT* IS THE QUESTION**

This necklace looks good either way. If you do opt to antique, the easiest way is to antique the finished chain before you embellish with the head-pin dangles. It makes the cleaning and polishing of the necklace easier to do. Antique the head pins separately and wrap them on after the necklace is polished.

EMBELLISH

Now you'll use the 4- to 6-mm beads. Place one on each balled head pin. Make a loop on each, but don't wrap them closed. Slip a number of them on in random clusters along the sections of chain, and check to see if you like the look. Once you do, attach them with a final wrap. Also attach a charm to each cluster of embellishment, using a jump ring ⑦.

Tip: I don't usually add any embellishment to the sections of chain closest to the clasp, because they can get caught in hair and don't really show anyway. Adding more than the 20-odd dangles and charms described in the previous paragraph is perfectly fine and can make for an interesting effect.

CLASP

8 Make a wrapped eye loop on one end of the 14-gauge wire 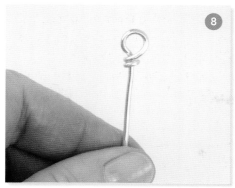.

9 Slide on the silver bead and push it against the top of the wire wrap. Using flat-nose pliers, bend a 45° angle in the wire, right against the bead .

10 Forge ½ inch (1.3 cm) of the end of the wire paper thin .

11 Use your small round-nose pliers to make a loop at the end of the forged wire. This loop should be a rotation and a half. Make sure you orient it as shown in 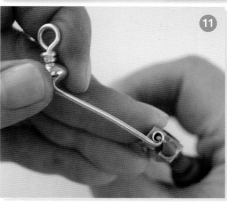.

12 Use the multibarrel pliers to form a hook 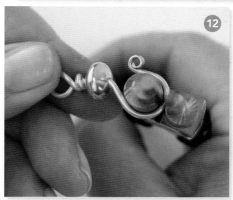. Finish the clasp by forging the top of the curve of the hook .

13 Attach the clasp to either end of the chain, using the 7-mm jump ring.

All that's left is to make yourself some matching earrings, then go out and show off your work!

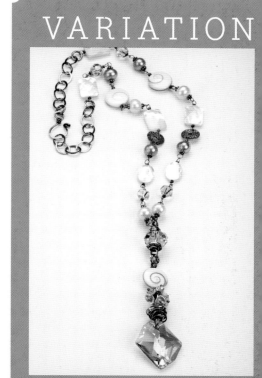

VARIATION

CLAMSHELL EARRINGS

by Janice Berkebile — Spiral away to create these spellbinding earrings!

YOU'LL NEED

16 inches (40.6 cm) of 16-gauge sterling silver wire

2 pearls, 8 to 12 mm

Two 22-gauge balled head pins, 3 inches long

2 ear wires

Liver of sulfur

Ruler

Flush wire cutters

Round-nose pliers

Chain-nose pliers

1 Antique the wire and cut it in half. Flush-cut both ends of both pieces.

2 Using the bottom quarter of the round-nose pliers, make a spiral four full revolutions long on the end of one wire 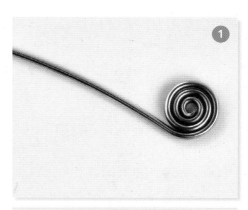. Repeat with the second wire.

3 On the other end of one wire, make a spiral that faces the opposite direction as the first, and that's also four full revolutions long 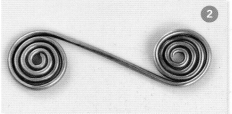. Do the same to the second wire.

4 On one wire, insert the round-nose pliers into the center of a spiral and push out to create a hollow area . Working from the same side, insert the round-nose pliers into the center of the other spiral and push out. Repeat on the second wire.

5 Next, you'll bend the wire to create a clamshell form. Grip the base of a spiral with the chain-nose pliers and hold the other spiral on that wire between your thumb and index. Rotate your hand to bend the spirals slightly toward each other 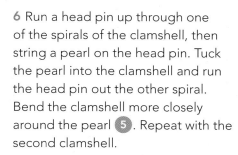. Repeat with the other wire.

6 Run a head pin up through one of the spirals of the clamshell, then string a pearl on the head pin. Tuck the pearl into the clamshell and run the head pin out the other spiral. Bend the clamshell more closely around the pearl . Repeat with the second clamshell.

7 On the end of the head pin, make a double-loop eye against the spiral on the clamshell . Flush-cut the extra wire. Repeat on the second clamshell.

8 Attach an ear wire to each double-eye loop.

SPIRAL LINK BRACELET

by Janice Berkebile A couple of twists take spirals to a whole new level. Just a slight change in the link design and—presto!—you've got a matching clasp. Create a strong bracelet with these handsome links and some of your favorite beads.

YOU'LL NEED

26½ inches (67.3 cm) of 14-gauge dead-soft copper wire

18 inches (45.7 cm) of 18-gauge dead-soft copper wire

4 semiprecious beads, 10 mm

Liver of sulfur

Round-nose pliers

Chain-nose pliers

Flush wire cutters

Long round-nose pliers

Chasing hammer

Bench block and pad

SPIRAL LINK

1 Make three spiral links by following steps 1 to 7. For each link, cut 5 inches (12.7 cm) of 14-gauge wire. Flush-cut both ends.

2 Working at the bottom quarter of the round-nose pliers, grip the end of the wire and form a spiral that has three full revolutions ❶.

Tip: Because the wire is quite thick, it's best to start the spiral further down on the plier. Begin by tapering the spiral, then form an initial circle that's as small as possible.

3 Hammer the entire spiral to strengthen it, but avoid forging the part of the wire that hasn't yet been formed ❷.

4 Working three-quarters of the way up the round-nose pliers and about ½ inch (1.3 cm) away from the top of the spiral, begin to roll the tail end of the wire around the tool ❸. Stop when you're just above the top of the spiral.

5 Leaving the pliers in position, close the loop by using your other hand to bring the wire over and across the top of the other wire so it's at a 90° angle to the spiral ❹.

6 Hold onto the spiral and the remaining wire with chain-nose pliers and shape the wire, little by little, halfway around the spiral ❺.

7 Forge the part of the wire shaped in step 6, avoiding the loop ❻.

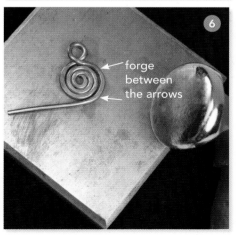

forge between the arrows

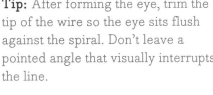

8 Using the base of the long round-nose plier, form an eye opposite the loop **7**.

Tip: After forming the eye, trim the tip of the wire so the eye sits flush against the spiral. Don't leave a pointed angle that visually interrupts the line.

. . . .

SPIRAL CLASP

9 Using 5½ (14 cm) inches of 14-gauge wire, follow steps 2 through 7.

10 Make the eye as described in step 8, except use the base of the long round-nose pliers to create a larger eye than on the links **8**.

11 Hold the spiral with the flat-nose pliers and rotate the eye a quarter turn, so it sits perpendicular to the spiral **9**. This is the eye into which the hook of the clasp will connect. Set it aside.

12 Using 6 inches (15.2 cm) of 14-gauge wire, follow steps 2 through 7.

13 At the end of the wire, make a small loop that faces the spiral link **10**.

14 Grip the wire at the base of the long round-nose pliers, with the tool sitting right next to the initial loop and the loop facing you **11**. Make a hook by rolling the tool toward the spiral **12**.

15 Hammer the hook to facet and strengthen the wire **13**.

LOOP-WRAPPED BEAD

16 You'll make four of these. For each, start with 2½ inches (6.4 cm) of 18-gauge wire. Spiral in both ends of the wire, in opposite directions, two full revolutions **14**.

17 Using the chain-nose pliers, bend the spirals slightly inward, so they face each other with a gentle curve **15**. Set them aside.

18 Make four eye pins, each 2 inches (5.1 cm) long **16**.

19 Slide one end of an element set aside in step 17 onto an eye pin, through the center of the spiral. Slide on a bead. Poke the eye pin through the center of the opposite spiral **17**.

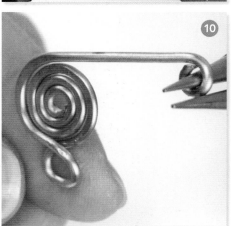

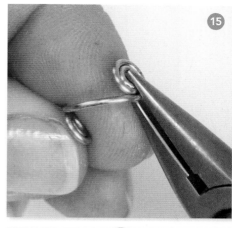

20 Finish by forming an eye on the other side .

ASSEMBLE AND FINISH

21 Using the eyes of the loop-wrapped beads, make a chain of alternating loop-wrapped beads and spiral links that begins and ends with loop-wrapped beads.

22 Attach half the clasp at one end and the other part of the clasp on the opposite end.

23 Dip the piece in liver of sulfur, shine it up, and you're on your way.

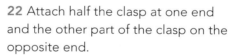

MY BEACH BRACELET

by Tracy Stanley

Gathering the materials for this bracelet can be your own
personal beachcombing moment. Wearing it will remind
you of cool ocean breezes and sand between your toes.

YOU'LL NEED

3 feet (91.4 cm) of 24-gauge dead-soft sterling silver wire

3 feet (91.4 cm) of 22-gauge dead-soft sterling silver wire

4 inches (10.2 cm) of 14-gauge dead-soft sterling silver wire

1 silver bead, ½ inch (1.3 cm) long

1 beach-themed sterling silver charm

6 crystals, pearls, or mother-of-pearl beads, 8 or 9 mm*

8 crystals, pearls, or mother-of-pearl beads, 4 mm*

4 crystals or pearls, 6 mm*

1 bead cap or puka shell with hole*

1 coin-shaped shell bead, ¾ inch (1.9 cm) in diameter*

1 coin-shaped shell bead, ½ inch (1.3 cm) in diameter*

1 faceted mother-of-pearl rectangular bead, ¾ x ½ inch (1.9 x 1.3 cm) *

2 faceted crystal or stone rondelles, 14 to 15 mm*

1 top-drilled mother-of-pearl bead*

12 silver spacers, 4 to 10 mm

1 soldered forged ring, 10 mm inside diameter

2 soldered forged rings, 7 mm inside diameter

6 balled head pins, 24 gauge

3 sterling silver jump rings, 7 mm inside diameter

Small round-nose pliers

Chain-nose pliers

Flat-nose pliers

Flush wire cutters

Small multibarrel pliers

Chasing hammer

Bench block and pad

See box at top right

COLLECTING YOUR BEADS

When choosing beads for this bracelet, look for things with different finishes—faceted, transparent, opaque, glass, and silver, for example. I prefer to use pearls, shell beads, mother-of-pearl, quartz, and crystals.

BEAD STRANDS

You'll start this bracelet in the center and work to the ends. Each side has two strands. One of them contains the larger beads while the other consists of all small beads. The order in which you add beads to each strand isn't important. Just make sure that you balance the sides by using beads of similar sizes and weights on each strand.

. . . .

Tip: Use the heavier of the wires—the 24- or 22-gauge—that will fit through the beads you're putting on. Work with wire cut to lengths of about 1 foot (30.5 cm). Wire-wrap a bead, cut it off, and continue to use the wire until you run out. This actually saves wire. If you try to guess how much wire you need for each bead, you'll almost always have waste.

. . . .

1 Cut a foot (30.5 cm) of wire. Make a loop 1 inch (2.5 cm) from one end of the wire, and slide it onto the large forged ring (which will be at the center of the finished bracelet), as shown in 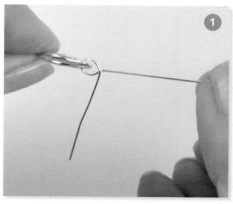. Finish the loop as a wrapped eye loop.

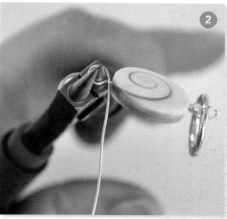

2 Put on one of the large coin-shaped beads and make a loop on the other side ❷, then finish the loop as a wrapped eye loop and trim the wire.

3 Make your next loop and connect it to the previous loop before turning it into a wrapped eye loop.

4 Repeat steps 2 and 3 to make a 6-inch-long (15.2 cm) strand of wrapped eye loops with beads. (Use the 4- to 10-mm spacers on the ends of some of the beads as you make your strand.) Before closing the last wrapped eye loop, attach one of the small forged rings to it.

5 Repeat steps 1 through 4 to create another strand of large beads and attach it to the large forged ring that serves as the center of the bracelet .

6 Next, make two strands with the smaller beads, making sure to catch one end of each in the larger forged ring and one end of each in either of the smaller rings. You'll note in ④ that I like to put these strands on opposite sides of the larger strands—so in the photo, one strand is at bottom left and the other strand is at top right, on the other side of the large forged ring.

EMBELLISHMENTS

The large forged ring can be embellished with dangles of beads on head pins, top-drilled beads, and/ or charms. These pieces will all be put on later with jump rings so you don't need to worry about attaching them before you close the loops.

TOP-DRILLED BEAD

8 Put the wire through the bead with about 1 inch (2.5 cm) of wire sticking out one side **5**.

9 Bend both sides of the wire up toward the tip of the bead **6**.

10 Using flat-nose pliers, make an angle in the longer of the wire ends, just above the tip of the bead **7**.

11 Fold the shorter wire over the angled bend in the longer wire **8**, then wrap the shorter wire around the longer wire. Trim off any extra wire **9**.

12 Using round-nose pliers and the long wire, make a loop that sits right above the wrapped wire **10**. Wrap the loop closed, and continue wrapping until you reach the top of the bead **11**. If you have enough wire, make a second layer of wrapping over the first, ending just under the loop **12**. This gives a thicker appearance to the wired area between the loop and the bead. Trim off any extra wire.

DANGLES

Place a bead on each of the head pins and wire-wrap them closed **13**.

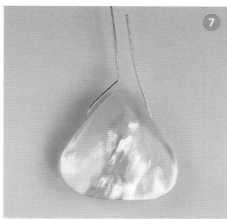

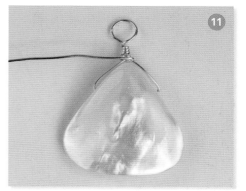

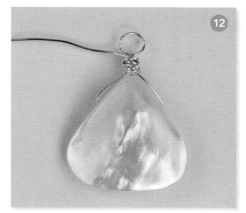

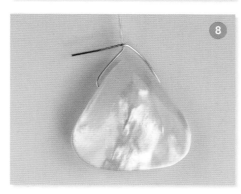

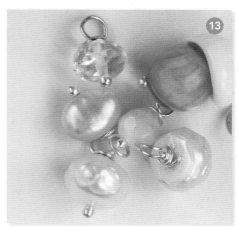

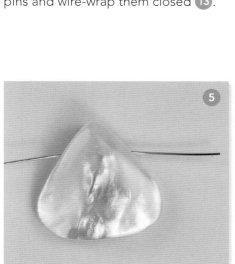

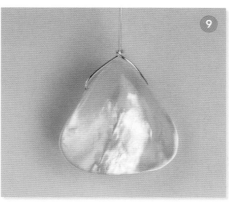

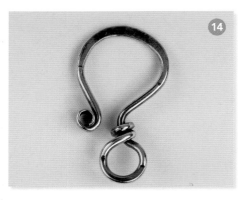

CLASP

Use the 14-gauge wire to make a hook clasp  14 .

FINISH

13 Open one of the jump rings using a chain-nose and flat-nose pliers. Put on the wrapped top-drilled bead and all of the dangle beads you've made 15 . Hook the jump ring to the large forged ring 16 and close the jump ring.

14 Attach the charm to the large forged ring using a jump ring 17 .

15 Using a jump ring, attach the clasp to one of the smaller forged rings on the end of the bracelet 18 . If the bracelet isn't long enough, add more linked jump rings to the end before attaching the clasp.

Put your bracelet on. Listen closely. Can't you just about hear the pounding of the surf?

BEACH PEBBLE BRACELET

by Janice Berkebile

Simple wire techniques and drilled pebbles combine to create this captivating bracelet. The smoothly polished pebbles evoke the tranquility of the beach.

YOU'LL NEED

54 inches (1.4 m) of 16-gauge dead-soft sterling silver wire

25 inches (63.5 cm) of 14-gauge dead-soft sterling silver wire

2 sterling silver charms*

9 to 12 roundish center-drilled pebbles, 12–17 mm

9 to 11 top-drilled pebbles, 6–10 mm long

Liver of sulfur

Ruler

Flush wire cutters

Chasing hammer

Bench block and pad

Long round-nose pliers

Round-nose pliers

Multibarrel pliers

Chain-nose pliers

I use shell shapes.

PEBBLE CONNECTORS

1 The quantity of pebble connectors you'll need to make will vary, depending on your wrist size. (Nine are needed for a 6-inch [15.2 cm] wrist; adjust accordingly.) Each pebble connector requires two spiral spacers and one center-drilled pebble. Start by making the spiral spacers, as follows:

Cut a piece of 16-gauge wire 20 inches (50.8 cm) long. Working from one end, shape a spiral, making two full revolutions, then cut the wire at an angle **1**. Hammer the spacer to strengthen and texture it **2**. Using the leftover 16-gauge wire, make as many more spacers as needed, then set them aside.

. . . .

Tip: These little spiral spacers will fly away while you hammer unless you tape or hold them down.

. . . .

2 Set aside one pebble; you'll use it later to make a clasp connector.

3 Next, you'll assemble the eye loops for each pebble connector. Cut 18 inches (45.7 cm) of 14-gauge wire. Working from one end of the wire, make a loop halfway up the long round-nose pliers. Slide on a spiral spacer, with the textured side facing down. Add a pebble, and top it with a spiral spacer that's facing textured side up. Cut the wire to 1 inch (2.5 cm) and make a loop on the second side. The loops should open in opposite directions **3**. Forge the ends of all the loops and antique all the pebble connectors.

PERPENDICULAR FIGURE-EIGHT LOOPS

You'll use these to hang the drop pebbles later. Make as many loops as you have top-drilled pebbles.

4 Working off the end of the 16-gauge wire, form a figure-eight eye loop with perpendicular loops, forming one loop on the base of the round-nose pliers, and the other loop halfway up the round-nose pliers, so the loops are different sizes. Hammer the ends of all the loops and antique them **4**.

CLASP

Using 4 inches (10.2 cm) of 14-gauge wire, make a hook clasp with a wrapped loop and antique it. To make the spiral at the tip of the hook, work a quarter of the way up the round-nose pliers. Form the body of the hook on the middle tier of the multibarrel pliers. Form the loop around the round-nose pliers, halfway up **5**.

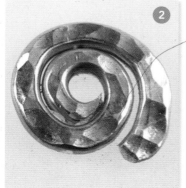

CLASP CONNECTOR

Remember that pebble you set aside in step 2? Using 2 to 3 inches (5.1 to 7.6 cm) of 14-gauge wire—depending on the thickness of the pebble—make a bead loop as described in step 3, with this exception: make one of the loops halfway up the pliers, and the other side on the base of the long round-nose pliers **6**. The loop on this side has to be large enough for the hook to pass through **7**. And, as for the pebble connectors, the loops should open in opposite directions. Hammer the loops to strengthen the wire.

ASSEMBLY

5 Opening the bead loops as needed, connect the pebble connectors together sequentially to form a chain. Attach the clasp connector on one end.

6 On the other end of the chain, add the two charms and then the hook clasp **8**.

7 To create a dangle, open one loop of a perpendicular figure-eight loop and attach a top-drilled pebble to it. Repeat to attach one pebble to each of the remaining figure-eight loops. Attach these dangles to every other loop of the pebble connectors, so the dangles all hang facing the same direction **9**.

WIRE-WRAPPED PENDANT

by Tracy Stanley

One of the trickiest beads to wrap is a flat pendant with a hole at the top. This project will show you how to turn a hard-to-use piece into a great pendant. Hunt for a dramatic chain or cord from which to hang it.

YOU'LL NEED

32 inches (81.3 cm) of 18-gauge dead-soft sterling silver wire

Top-drilled, flat teardrop-shaped stone pendant, 1¾ x 1½ inches (4.4 x 3.8 cm)*

1 faceted accent bead, 12 to 14 mm

14 to 16 embellishment beads, 4 to 8 mm

14 to 16 balled head pins, 24 gauge

3 spacer beads, 5 mm

One 14-gauge jump ring, 12 mm inside diameter

1 sterling silver bail, optional

Liver of sulfur

Long round-nose pliers

Short round-nose pliers

Chain-nose pliers

Flat-nose pliers

Flush wire cutters

Measuring tape

Chasing hammer

Bench block and pad

*This bead can have a hole that goes straight through from front to back, or one that goes from edge to edge. The latter style of hole tends to be smaller and may require you to use a thinner wire to wrap with. Some stones can be reamed out, making the hole larger, but you always risk breaking the bead. It's okay to use a larger or smaller pendant bead, but it's important that its shape be a flattened teardrop.

PENDANT

1 Cut 20 inches (50.8 cm) of 18-gauge wire and place the teardrop-shaped pendant bead on it, leaving roughly 2 inches (5.1 cm) of wire sticking out of one end **1**.

2 Fold both ends of the wire up **2**. Near the tip of the bead, bend a slight angle in the longer side of the wire, using your flat-nose pliers **3**.

3 Using your hand, fold the shorter side of the wire over to the other side of the bead **4**. Wrap the shorter end tight around the longer wire for one full rotation **5**, then cut off any extra wire **6**.

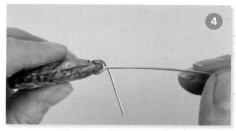

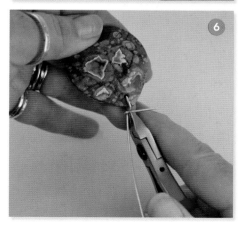

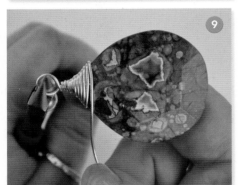

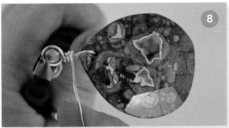

4 Using round-nose pliers and the long side of the wire, make a loop just above the single wrap you just made  **7** . Holding the piece by the loop and using the same wire, wrap it several times below the loop **8** and cap the bead at least as far as the hole **9** . At a certain point it may be easier to take the round-nose pliers out of the loop and wrap the wire while holding the pendant in your hand. If in step 5 you want to make an open spiral on the front of your bead, as shown here (you can opt not to), you should retain at least 2 to 3 inches (5.1 to 7.6 cm) of unwrapped wire.

5 To make the open spiral, trim the wire down to between 2 and 3 inches (5.1 to 7.6 cm)—the amount depends on the size of your bead and how big you want the spiral to be. Using round-nose pliers, make a loop on the end of the wire **10**, then use all the rest of the wire to shape a flat spiral positioned at the center of one side of the bead **11** . Gently pull the spiral away from the bead, place it on your bench block, and flatten and shape it with a chasing hammer **12**. Fold the spiral back into place with your chain nose pliers. Antique and polish this pendant.

DOUBLE-LOOP WRAPPED ACCENT BEAD

6 Beginning 3 inches (7.6 cm) from the end, make a double-loop eye wrap on the end of a 12-inch (30.5 cm) piece of 18-gauge wire. Slide on the accent bead and make a double-loop eye wrap on the other end. Don't trim off the extra wire at this point. Beginning on the side with the shortest wire, make a spiral cap on this end of the bead. Then, with the longer wire, make a cap on the second side. Don't trim the extra wire off yet. You'll need it for the next step.

7 Bring the extra wire around the bead **13** and wrap the end around the loop on the other side of the bead **14**. Trim off any extra wire, and antique and polish this component.

EMBELLISHMENT BEADS

8 Slide one embellishment bead on each balled head pin (for the three largest beads, add a spacer to the head pin first, then put on the bead), and make a wrapped eye loop with or without spiral cap to hold the beads on the head pins.

9 Antique and clean up these components **15**.

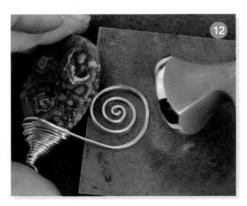

ASSEMBLE

10 Open the jump ring and put your pendant on it. Next, place on the embellishment beads , putting the larger ones on first and then the smaller ones. This will make the cluster look more balanced. Finally, slide on the double-loop wrapped accent bead.

11 Close the jump ring with chain nose and flat nose pliers .
Optional: Attach a bail to the loop of the double-loop wrapped accent bead that has nothing attached to it; this will allow you to slide your piece onto thicker chain. If you don't have or don't want a bail, that's okay. Just run a chain or a cord through the free loop of the double-loop wrapped accent bead and your pendant is ready to wear.

You can dangle this pendant from any of the chains that this book teaches. Mix it up and have some fun!

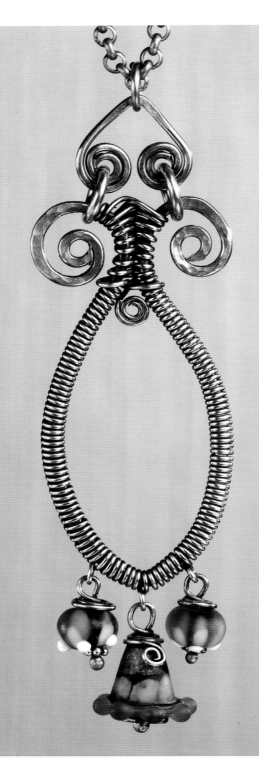

COILED DROP PENDANT

by Janice Berkebile — Coil yourself a beautiful frame to complement some spectacular beads. You'll be happy wearing this gorgeous pendant!

YOU'LL NEED

8 inches (20.3 cm) of 14-gauge dead-soft copper wire

5 feet (1.5 m) of 20-gauge dead-soft copper wire

6 inches (15.2 cm) of 16-gauge dead-soft copper wire

1 cone-shaped lampwork bead, 12 x 15 mm

2 complementary beads, 8 mm

2 sterling silver spacers, 3 mm

Two 14-gauge jump rings, 6 mm

Liver of sulfur

Round-nose pliers

Chain-nose pliers

Permanent marker

Ruler

Flush wire cutters

Chasing hammer

Bench pad and block

Tweezers

Butane torch

A fireproof surface

Small bowl of water

FOUNDATION

1 On both ends of the 14-gauge wire, make open spirals that face the same direction ①.

2 Mark the center of the wire. Place the side of the chain-nose pliers just to the right of the mark. With your thumb on the left side, push the wire against the edge of the plier to form an angle.

3 Using chain-nose pliers, hold the bottom of the piece right next to the angle you just made. With your thumb, push the wire out to make a nice smooth curve that's identical on both sides ②.

4 Hammer the foundation piece to strengthen it ③, then texture the spirals with the peen side of the hammer ④.

COIL

5 As shown in ⑤, make a mark near the spirals for the coil's start and stop points. Also make marks near the bend where the loops will go.

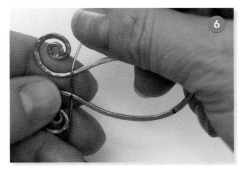

6 Cut 4 feet (1.2 m) of 20-gauge wire. Leaving a 2-inch (5.1 cm) tail, place the coiling wire over the framing wire on the right side of the foundation piece, at the uppermost mark ⑥. Holding the top right spiral in your left hand,

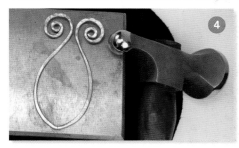

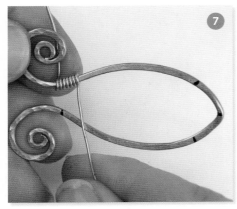

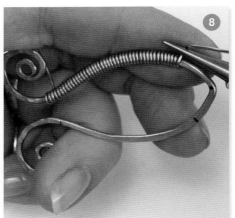

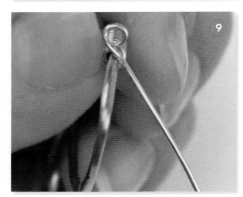

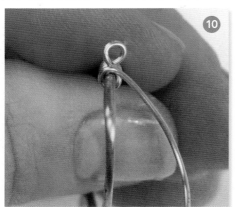

start wrapping the right side of the piece, allowing the coiling wire to pass between the two spirals as you work 7. Coil to the next mark.

. . . .

Tip: Take your time wrapping; 20-gauge is a strong wire, and you want to achieve a nice, clean wrap with no gaps.

. . . .

7 At the mark, you need to make what I call a gypsy wire wrap. To do so, place the round-nose pliers against the coiling wire, on the exterior of the curve of the foundation 8. With the forefinger of the left hand, bring the wire back in the direction opposite the direction in which you were coiling and around the pliers, to form a loop. The loop should rest against the foundation wire. Pull the wire up over the framework and remove the pliers 9. You're now in position to continue coiling as before 10.

. . . .

Tip: This way of making a loop hides the wire because it's done in a figure-eight fashion rather than just coiling over two pieces of framing wire, which would leave the coiling wire visible. Since I view my method as more than a loop, I gave it a special name: a gypsy wire wrap.

. . . .

8 To make the second loop, coil to the next mark, repeat step 7, then coil to the next mark. Make a third loop as described in step 7, but feel free to tweak its placement so it balances visually with the first loop. Finally, coil the left side of the piece up to the mark near the spiral 11. Don't cut the wire.

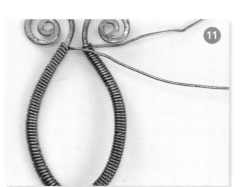

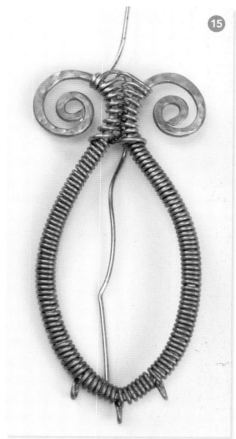

BASKET WEAVE

9 Take the working wire from the left side to the right side from behind, bringing it up over the front as shown in ⓬.

10 Weave the working wire around the foundation wire in a figure-eight fashion to bind the two sides together, as shown in ⓭ and ⓮, until you reach the top ⓯.

11 Wind the wire once more to secure it, and trim it in back.

12 Cut the tail so it's ¾ inch (1.9 cm) long and form it into a spiral tucked into the bottom of the basket weave ⓰.

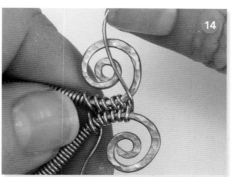

TRIANGLE CONNECTOR

Cut 3 inches (7.6 cm) of 16-gauge wire. On both ends, make spirals that face in and that are two full revolutions. Bend an angle at the center  and hammer the element to strengthen it.

SPIRAL SPACER

Cut 3 inches (7.6 cm) of 16-gauge wire. Working on the bottom quarter of the pliers, shape a closed spiral with a small hole at its center, making two full revolutions. Cut the end at an angle. Hammer the spiral to strengthen and texture it. Set it aside for now.

. . . .

Tip: While you hammer, this little spacer might fly away unless you tape or hold it down.

. . . .

DANGLES

13 Cut three pieces of 20-gauge wire, each 4 inches (10.2 cm) long. Use them to make balled head pins **18**.

14 Thread the spiral spacer and the tapered bead on a head pin. Attach it to the central loop using a wrapped eye loop with spiral cap. (If you like, you can make a spiral flourish using the end of the working wire, as shown in **19**.) On each of the remaining headpins thread a sterling silver spacer and a bead. Attach those to the loops on either side of the central one, again using a wrapped eye loop with spiral cap **20**.

FINISH

15 Attach the triangle connector to the top of the pendant, using the 6-mm jump rings **21**.

16 Antique the piece in liver of sulfur. Shine it up, dangle it from a chain or a ribbon, and enjoy!

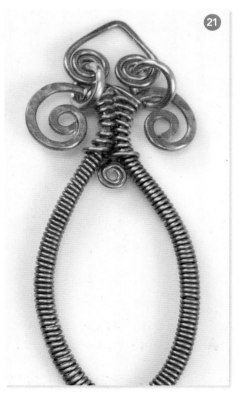

WIRE-WRAPPED BANGLE

A girl can *never* have too many bangles. Wear this one alone or in multiples. Solo or in quantity, the look is fabulous!

COILS

Coil the 18-gauge wire around the mandrel or the piece of copper 14-gauge wire. Slide the coil off ①.

CENTER SECTION

1 Cut a piece of silver 14-gauge wire 3½ inches (8.9 cm) long. Make sure each end is flush-cut. Make a mark ¾ inch (1.9 cm) from each end. Slide on a 12- to 14-mm bead ②. Slide an 8-mm spacer on each side of it.

2 Refer to ③ as you do this step. Slide a 10-mm bead beside each of the spacers, then add 6-mm spacers or beads on both sides of those. Center the beads along the wire and measure the space between the last spacer and the mark on the wire. Cut two section of coil to that length.

Tip: Here's how to cut small sections of coil without crushing the ends:
1 Measure the length of coil you want. Using your flush wire cutters, gently squeeze the coil to slightly open it in the spot you want to cut ④.
2 Cut off the coil section ⑤.
3 Trim both ends, to remove any sharp bits of metal ⑥. If you crush the ends, trim back the coil until what remains can slide easily onto the foundation wire (the 14-gauge wire).

3 Slide a coil on each end. Make sure the coils line up with the marks on the wire. Attach a piece of masking tape on one end ⑦ to keep your beads from falling off as you finish the other end in the next step.

4 Using round-nose pliers, make an eye loop from all the wire left at the end ⑧.

5 Remove the masking tape from the other side and make an eye on that end ⑨.

6 Using your chasing hammer, flatten the tops of both eyes ⑩.

SIDE SECTIONS

7 You'll need to make two of these. Refer to ⑪ as you do steps 7 to 11. For each one, cut a piece of 14-gauge wire 3½ inches (8.9 cm) long. Make a mark ¾ inch (1.9 cm) from each end. On each wire, place on a 12- to 14-mm bead. Slide an 8-mm spacer on each side of it, and an 8-mm bead on each side of the spacers. Cut a total of 4 coils, each ³⁄₁₆ inch (5 cm) long, and slide one on each end of both wires, to flank the 8-mm beads. Finally, put a 6-mm spacer on each end. Center all the beads on each wire.

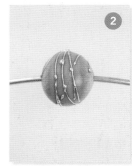

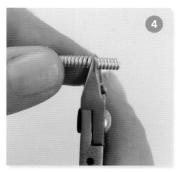

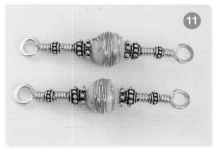

8 As you did for the center section, measure from the last beads or spacers to the marks on the ends of the wire, and cut coils to fit. Trim any sharp ends flush and slide the coils onto each end. Attach a piece of masking tape to one end of each wire, to keep your beads from falling off in the next step.

9 Make an eye loop on each end of the wire, removing the masking tape as necessary.

10 Forge the tops of the eyes.

FORM THE SECTIONS

11 Before assembling your bracelet, you need to form each section into a gentle curve. Do this by holding the eyes on both sides of each section and pulling down on them while pushing the center outward.

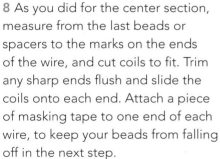

12 Use your flat-nose pliers to gently bend the eyes to match the curvature of the foundation wire . You'll be able to fine-tune the curves after you put the bangle together, so don't worry about making it perfect.

ASSEMBLE

13 Using a jump ring, attach your center section to one of the side sections  with their curves facing the same direction. Attach a second jump ring next to the first.

14 Repeat step 13 on the other side of the center section, attaching the second side section .

15 Attach three jump rings to each other in a chain; attach one end to one of the side sections, and the other end to the other side section, closing the bangle. At this point you can finish forming the curves by pulling the bangle into a nice round shape .

16 Try the bracelet on to see if or how it fits. What if it's too small? Add more single jump rings to lengthen the chain of three assembled in step 15, until the bangle slides on comfortably. What if it's too big? Remove some of the single jump rings from the chain made in step 15

until you're happy with the size of the bracelet.

. . . .

Tip: If your hand is just too large to make a bangle that looks good on your wrist, this piece can also be made with a clasp. You'll need to shorten the length of the two side sections by ½ inch (1.3 cm). Then make a clasp of your choice and attach it to either side section using the loop or a jump ring.

. . . .

DANGLES

17 Using 3 inches of silver 14-gauge wire, make an open spiral with perpendicular loop to use as a charm. Forge and texture it as desired.

18 Using one or several jump rings, attach all four charms to the chain .

The only thing left to do is put this bangle on your wrist and start making your next one! After all, one is never enough!

. . . .

Tip: The charms hanging from this area of the bangle will act as a counterbalance, keeping the back side of the bangle from rotating to the top.

. . . .

ENCRUSTED EARRINGS by Tracy Stanley

These earrings are fun to put together and even more fun to wear! Make them flashy by using lots of crystals, or tone them down by including elegant pearls. Either way—make them, wear them, and enjoy!

Tip: When choosing beads for these earrings, make sure you have two of each so that you can make a matching pair of earrings.

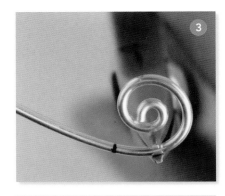

YOU'LL NEED

6 inches (15.2 cm) of 16-gauge dead-soft sterling silver wire

6 inches (15.2 cm) of 20-gauge dead-soft sterling silver wire

2 lampwork beads, 8 mm*

8 small- to medium-size keshi pearls, center drilled**

4 freshwater pearls, 6 mm**

2 faceted hematite (or other stone) beads, 6 mm**

8 faceted crystal rondelles, 4 mm**

12 faceted crystal bicones, 3 mm**

34 sterling silver balled head pins, 24 gauge

2 ear wires

Ruler

Flush wire cutters

Permanent marker

Small round-nose pliers

Chain-nose pliers

Flat-nose pliers

Chasing hammer

Block and pad

*Their holes must allow 16-gauge wire to pass through.

**You may substitute any beads of similar size.

1 Cut two pieces of 16-gauge wire, each 3 inches (7.6 cm) long. Mark the center of each piece **1**.

2 Using the small round-nose pliers, start an open spiral on one end of each of the wires by creating a loop **2**. Finish the spiral with chain-nose pliers. This spiral should end at the marked center point **3**.

3 Use flat-nose pliers to bend the wires at an angle just beyond the spiral, right on the mark **4**.

4 Flatten the spirals on the block, using the chasing hammer **5**.

5 Wrap the 20-gauge wire three times around each of the shaped 16-gauge wires, just above the angle **6**, then cut off the excess. If the mark on the wire still shows, scrub it off.

6 Place one of the 8-mm lampwork beads on each of the shaped 16-gauge wires **7**. Set aside.

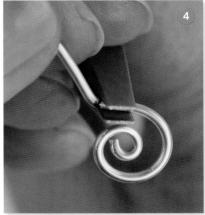

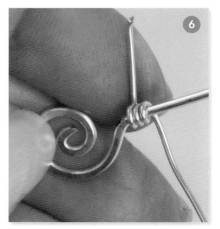

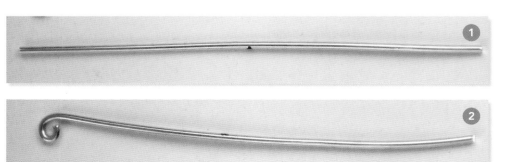

7 Place the remaining beads—one each—on the balled head pins and make a wrapped eye loop on each. Trim off any excess wire. Divide the wrapped beads equally and set half aside.

8 Slide half of the wrapped beads on one of the shaped 16-gauge wires, beginning with the larger ones and finishing with the smallest **8**.

9 Using the small round nose-pliers, make an eye loop on the end of the wire. This loop needs to end right above the wrapped beads to catch them tightly **9**. Attach an ear wire to the loop.

10 Assemble the second earring by repeating steps 8 and 9.

Now, put them on and enjoy the fruits of your labor!

VARIATION

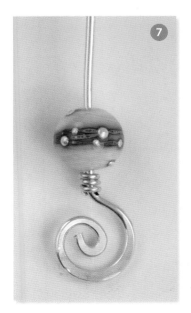

COILS AND BEADS BRACELET

by Tracy Stanley   This bracelet can show off beautiful lampwork beads. It's quick to make—and makes a statement!

4 feet (1.2 m) of 18-gauge dead-soft silver wire

15 inches (38.1 cm) of 14-gauge dead-soft copper wire

5 inches (12.7 cm) of 14-gauge dead-soft silver wire

1 bead, 16 mm*

2 beads, 14 mm*

2 beads, 10 mm*

2 bead caps (or spacers) to fit largest bead*

4 silver beads (or spacers), 6 mm*

6 silver spacers, 7 to 8 mm*

6 floater rings, 4-mm inside diameter (optional)**

Liver of sulfur

Mandrel, 14 gauge

Masking tape

Ruler

Flush wire cutters

Permanent marker

Long round-nose pliers

Small round-nose pliers

Chain-nose pliers

Chasing hammer

Bench block and pad

Multibarrel pliers

*Requires a hole that allows 14-gauge wire to pass through.

**If you can't find rings, you can make jump rings, to put on for movement

1 Coil all of the 18-gauge wire around the mandrel. (This can be done in one piece or in several.) Antique the coil and polish it.

2 Cut a piece of the 14-gauge copper wire 8 inches (20.3 cm) long. (This will be the foundation wire; if your wrist is larger than average, you may need to cut a longer piece.) Antique it. Mark 1 inch (2.5 cm) from each end.

Tip: Copper and silver don't like to antique once they're put together, so it's important to antique the foundation wire and the coils ahead of time. Cleanup is also much easier if antiquing is done before assembly.

3 Next, you'll put on the beads, working from the center out. Refer to **1** as you work steps 3 through 8. Begin by placing the largest bead on the wire and center it, then add a bead cap on each side of the bead. On each side of the bead caps, slide on a 6-mm silver bead. On each side, place a 14-mm bead and then a spacer.

Tip: You can change the sizes of the beads and spacers as desired. Simply add more or fewer beads and coils to reach an overall length of 6 inches (15.2 cm).

4 Cut two pieces of coil, each ½ inch (1.3 cm) long. Trim the ends of the coils and slide one on each end.

5 Slide a floater ring on each coil. (Doing this is optional, but it adds a nice bit of movement to the bracelet.)

6 On each side, place on a spacer and a 10-mm bead. Then put a spacer on each side.

7 Cut two pieces of coil, each ½ inch (1.3 cm) long. Trim the ends of the coils and slide one on each side. Put a floater ring on each coil (optional) and add a small silver bead on each end.

8 On each side, measure the length left between the small silver bead and the mark you made in step 2. Cut a piece of coil that length then slide it on the wire.

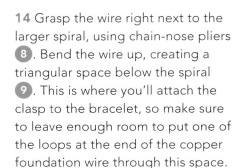

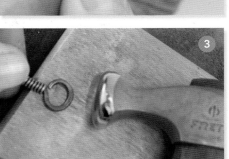

9 Attach a piece of masking tape on one end of the wire to prevent the beads from sliding off. On the other end make a loop, using the entire inch (2.5 cm) of visible wire **2**. Remove the masking tape and make a loop on that end of the wire, too.

10 Use the chasing hammer to flatten the top of the loops **3**, then use your hands to shape the bracelet to fit your wrist **4**.

Tip: Note the direction of the loops in the photo. Positioning the loops in this direction will allow the clasp to fit flat on the wrist.

SPIRAL CLASP

11 Forge one end of the 14-gauge silver wire flat **5**.

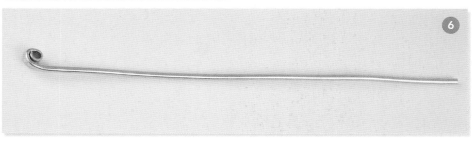

12 Using the small round-nose pliers, make a loop of one and a half rotations on the flattened end **6**.

13 On the other end of the wire, make a loop facing the same side of the wire as the first loop. Squeeze in this loop, using chain-nose pliers, then form it into a closed spiral until the total length of the element measures 2½ inches (6.4 cm) **7**.

14 Grasp the wire right next to the larger spiral, using chain-nose pliers **8**. Bend the wire up, creating a triangular space below the spiral **9**. This is where you'll attach the clasp to the bracelet, so make sure to leave enough room to put one of the loops at the end of the copper foundation wire through this space.

15 Shape the rest of the wire around the spiral as shown in **10**.

16 Using multibarrel pliers or long round-nose pliers, shape the hook as shown in **11**. Once you're happy with the shape of the hook, use the chasing hammer to flatten the top of it **12**. Also flatten the larger spiral; this will not only shape it, but remove any marks made while forming it **13**.

17 Antique and clean the clasp.

18 Open the loop on one end of the bracelet and slide the clasp into it **14**. Close the loop.

Tip: If the bracelet is too small, you can add jump rings at the end to attach the clasp. You may need to change the direction of the loops on the copper foundation wire so that the clasp rests flat against the wrist.

Now that you're finished, make a couple of companion bracelets, using some complementary lampwork beads. The All in One Wire-Wrapped Bracelet is a great bracelet to wear with this one!

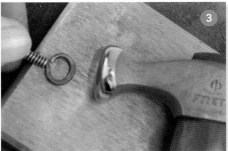

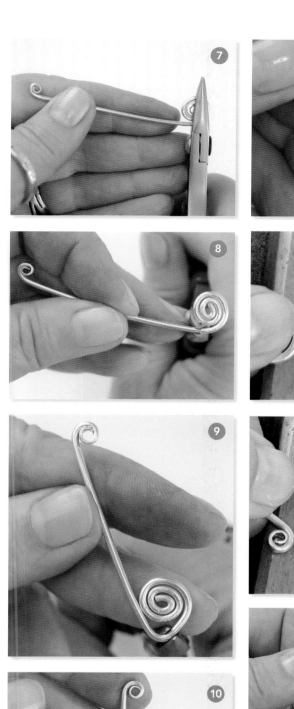

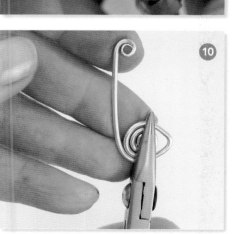

ALL IN ONE WIRE-WRAPPED BRACELET

by Tracy Stanley

You'll use the same piece of wire to create not only the foundation for the bracelet, but the clasp, too. Wear bunches of these bracelets!

YOU'LL NEED

5 feet (1.5 m) of 18-gauge dead-soft sterling silver wire

13 inches (33 cm) of 14-gauge dead-soft copper wire*

2 silver beads, 6 mm**

14 silver spacers, 6 to 7 mm**

7 glass, stone, or pearl beads, 10 to 12 mm**

Liver of sulfur

Ruler

Marker

14-gauge mandrel or 6 inches (15.2 cm) of 14-gauge wire

Flat-nose pliers

Chain-nose pliers

Chasing hammer

Bench block and pad

Long round-nose pliers

Flush wire cutters

*This is enough for a wrist 7 inches (17.8 cm) around or smaller. For a larger wrist, use more wire.

**All beads and spacers must have holes large enough to insert 14-gauge wire.

COILS

1 Coil the 18-gauge wire around the 14-gauge mandrel or the 6 inches (15.2 cm) of mandrel wire. (This can be done in one long piece, or in several pieces.)

2 Slide the coils off the 14-gauge wire and antique them, then set them aside.

CLASP HOOK

3 You'll start by forming the hook for the clasp. Mark one end of the 14-gauge wire in two places: 1 inch (2.5 cm) from the end and 2 inches (5.1 cm) from the end 1.

4 Using the flat-nose pliers, fold over the end of the wire at the 2-inch (5.1 cm) mark 2. Squeeze the fold tightly with the same tool 3.

5 Grasp the 1-inch (2.5 cm) mark with the flat-nose pliers and bend the wire at a right angle at that point; the bent wire should be in front, with the straight wire behind it 4.

6 Holding the folded wire close to the bend with the flat-nose pliers, grab the end of the wire with the chain-nose pliers 5 and wrap it tightly around the wire, as shown in 6 and 7.

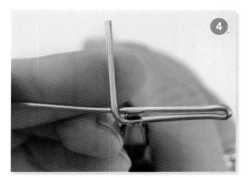

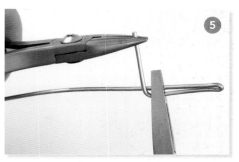

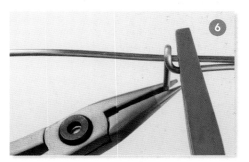

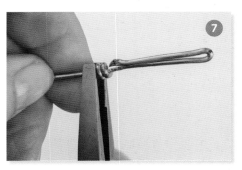

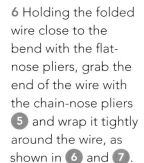

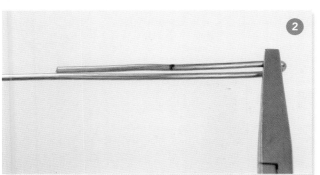

7 Forge the piece slightly to flatten the top of the fold .

8 Use the round-nose pliers to shape a hook 9. Bend up the end, using both the flat-nose and chain-nose pliers 10 and 11.

9 Antique this element.

ADD BEADS

The following measurements can change, depending on the size of your beads and the length of the foundation wire (the copper wire). If you need more or less coiled area, it's easiest to adjust for the difference on the ends.

10 Cut pieces of coil (made at the very beginning) to the following lengths:
- 2 sections ½ inch (1.3 cm) long
- 2 sections ⅜ inch (1 cm) long
- 6 sections ¼ inch (6 mm) long

11 Mark the unshaped end of the foundation wire 2½ inches (6.4 cm) from the tip.

12 As you do this step and the next two, refer to 12. Slide a ½-inch (1.3 cm) coil onto the foundation wire, then one of the 6-mm silver beads. Next put on a ⅜-inch (1 cm) coil, then a spacer, and finally a glass, stone, or pearl bead.

13 Add a spacer, a ¼-inch (6 mm) section of coil, another spacer, and a glass, stone, or pearl bead. Repeat until you've using all the beads.

14 Slide on the last spacer. Add the remaining ⅜-inch (1 cm) coil, the remaining 6-mm bead, and the last ½-inch (1.3 cm) coil.

· ·

Tip: You'll need at least 2½ inches (6.4 cm) of wire without beads on it to shape the loop for the clasp. You can form the bracelet over your wrist and give it a "test drive," trying it on to check the size and fit. If it's too big, take off some coils and trim them down. If it's too small, you may want to use smaller beads and more coils, or start over with a longer piece of 14-gauge wire and extra coils.

· ·

FINISH

15 Using the long round-nose pliers, grasp the foundation wire against the last coil that was added **13**. Fold over the wire **14** and form a large wrapped eye loop. Trim off any extra wire **15**.

16 Squeeze the tip of the wire so that it rests tightly against the curve of the coil then forge the end of the loop with the chasing hammer **16**.

17 Using your hands, gently shape the bracelet **17**. Before putting on the bracelet, you should make sure the clasp hook, which faces out, works smoothly, so test it in the loop. You may need to use flat-nose pliers to get the right angle on the loop or hook end.

So what are you waiting for? Make yourself a couple more!

CASCADING WATERFALL
GEMS PENDANT

by Janice Berkebile Frame a focal bead in coiled wire and embellish
the chain with sparkling gemstones. You'll bewitch
everyone with this dazzling pendant!

YOU'LL NEED

8 inches (20.3 cm) of 18-gauge dead-soft sterling silver wire

30 inches (76.2 cm) of 22-gauge dead-soft sterling silver wire

3 inches (7.6 cm) of 20-gauge dead-soft sterling silver wire

1½ inches (3.8 cm) of 16-gauge dead-soft sterling silver wire

1 charoite focal bead, 18 x 25 mm

1 ruby teardrop, 15 x 10 mm

2 green amethyst rondelles, 8 x 6 mm

4 chartreuse seed pearls, 3 mm

4 faceted garnet beads, 3 mm

1 amethyst rondelle, 6 mm

6 inches (15.2 cm) of silver chain*

Three 16-gauge silver jump rings, 6 mm

Twelve 24-gauge silver head pins, 2 inches (5.1 cm) long

Liver of sulfur

Round-nose pliers

Chasing hammer

Bench block and pad

Ruler

Permanent marker

Flush wire cutters

Chain-nose pliers

Flat-nose pliers

Long round-nose pliers

*See the tip box in the next column.

Tip: Choosing Chain

Choose medium-size chain that will be in scale with the piece. The chain you select doesn't have to be the same type for all three dangles. Choose at least 2 inches (5.1 cm) of a complex chain for the center and at least 2 inches (5.1 cm) of a simpler chain for each of the exteriors.

FRAMEWORK

1 Bring the two ends of the 18-gauge wire together and then cross them over each other. Pull each end away from the other to form a teardrop shape about ¼ inch (6 mm) long in the center of the wire **1** .

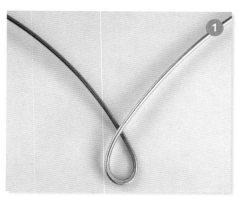

2 Hammer the bottom of the teardrop to strengthen it. *Don't* hammer the area where the wires cross; the wire will get weakened and it will break.

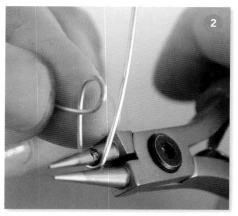

3 Hold the teardrop shape in your non-dominant hand, facing up, and use the round-nose pliers to grasp the wire about ½ inch (1.3 cm) away from the teardrop. Push the working wire up as shown in **2** . Roll in the pliers to create a loop about ¼ inch (6 mm) from the teardrop **3** .

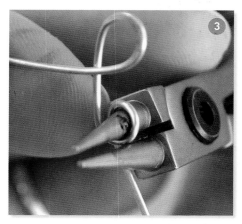

4 Repeat step 3 on the other side of the teardrop to create a second loop, bringing the wire around in the opposite direction **4** .

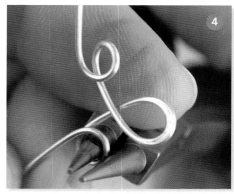

SUSPEND THE CHAIN

5 Slide the complex chain (if you opted for several types of chain) over the end of the wire, through the loop, and into the teardrop ❺.

Tip: If the chain doesn't have the same type of link along its entire length, you'll have to consider which direction the chain will face. Make sure to slide it on using the right link to make the visually more interesting side of the chain face out.

6 Holding the chain taut, measure and cut it 2 inches (5.1 cm) below the wire from which it dangles.

7 Slide the simpler style of chain on one of the loops, and, holding the chain taut, measure and cut it so it's 2 inches (5.1 cm) long. Repeat on the other loop ❻.

Tip: If the chain link is too small to get over the 18-gauge wire, widen the link by placing the round-nose pliers into it, then gently push it open.

MOUNT THE FOCAL BEAD

8 Coil the 22-gauge wire, using some 18-gauge wire as a mandrel. Cut the coil in half. Each coil should be 1¾ inches (4.4 cm) long.

9 Slide the coils onto the framework; push them all the way down to the top of the loops on both sides ❼. Set aside.

10 Slide the focal bead onto the 20-gauge wire and create an eye loop on each side. (Each eye should be large enough to just fit over the coils made in step 8.) Slide the eye loops over the coils of the framework. Holding the focal bead in position, crimp the eye pins gently to hold the focal bead in place ❽.

11 Shape the top of the frame to hug the focal bead ❾.

12 Form a spiral from the inch (2.5 cm) of wire remaining at the top of each side ❿. The holes of the spirals should be large enough to fit a jump ring through them. Set aside.

CONNECTOR

13 Use round-nose pliers to create identical loops that face the same way at both ends of the 16-gauge wire. Place the chain-nose pliers just to the right of the center of the wire and press the wire into the pliers to bend it at a crisp angle, like a V. Hammer the top and the bottom loops ⑪.

14 Connect the loops of the connector to the spirals at the top of the frame using two jump rings.

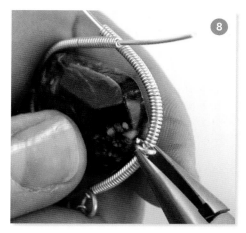

EMBELLISH

15 Antique the framework then clean it up before embellishing it.

16 Use wrapped eye loops with spiral caps to attach the ruby teardrop to the end of the focal chain . Use the same method to attach the larger amethyst rondelles to both of the outer chains.

17 Use wrapped eye loops with spiral caps to embellish the chain with dangles made from the remaining pearls and stones, as follows: Attach three beads each on the outer chains, ½ inch (1.3 cm) up from the beads attached in the previous step. On the central chain, add a bead to the fourth link from the wire teardrop, and add two beads to the fifth link from the wire teardrop.

MAKING WIRE & BEAD JEWELRY 89

GYPSY WIRE PENDANT

by Janice Berkebile Get your swagger on with this spectacular pendant dripping
with gemstones and pearls. Simply enchanting!

YOU'LL NEED

21 inches (53.3 cm) of 16-gauge dead-soft copper wire

107 inches (2.7 m) of 24-gauge dead-soft copper wire

5 brown pearls, 3 mm

5 faceted green garnet beads, 4 mm

2 ruby beads, 6 mm

1 faceted ruby bead, 7 mm

Six 16-gauge jump rings, 4 mm

One 14-gauge jump ring, 6 mm

Fifteen 24-gauge copper head pins

Liver of sulfur

Flush wire cutters

Ruler

Round-nose pliers

Large multibarrel pliers

Chasing hammer

Bench block and pad

Permanent marker

Chain-nose pliers

Long round-nose pliers

Flat-nose pliers

Flush wire cutters

Tweezers

Butane torch

A fireproof surface

Small bowl of water

FRAMES

Although they're different sizes, the shapes of the three tiers are essentially the same.

TOP TIER

1 Cut 3½ inches (8.9 cm) of 16-gauge wire.

2 Working halfway up the tip of the round-nose pliers, grasp the end of the wire with the tool and make a loop ❶. Make a second loop that faces in the same direction on the other end of the wire.

3 Grasp the wire in the base of the pliers and form it around the tool to make a second arc, as shown in ❷. Repeat on the other end of the wire ❸.

4 Grasp the center of the wire in the base of the long round-nose pliers and bend the loops toward each other over the pliers ❹.

MIDDLE TIER

5 Cut 4½ inches (11.4 cm) of 16-gauge wire.

6 Using this longer piece of wire, repeat steps 2 through 4 to create a frame similar to the top tier, but in the last step use the bottom section of the multibarrel pliers to form a larger curve in the center ❺.

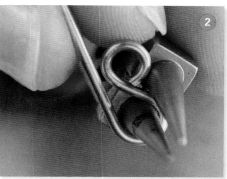

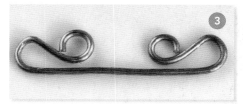

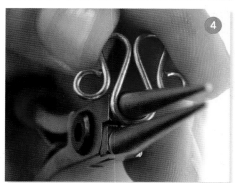

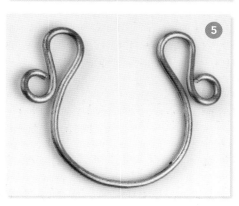

BOTTOM TIER

7 Cut 5½ inches (14 cm) of 16-gauge wire.

8 Using this wire, again repeat steps 2 through 4 to make a form that looks similar to the top tier, except in the last step, use the bottom tier of the multibarrel pliers to form an even larger curve in the center. As shown in 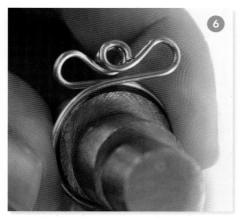, the two sides of the wire will overlap while being formed over the pliers.

9 Take the wirework off the pliers and gently pull the two sides away from each other 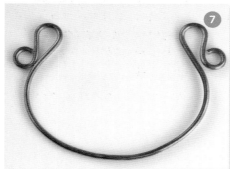.

FINE TUNE

10 Now you'll tweak the shapes of the tiers. Arrange them one below the next. First, examine how they relate to one another; they should nest. Use chain nose pliers to adjust the forms. Then look at the form of each one. They should all resemble each other. After you're done tweaking them, the forms should look like 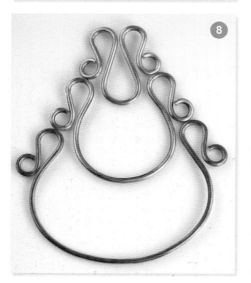.

11 Once you're done adjusting the pieces, forge the bottom, the top, and the two outside loops 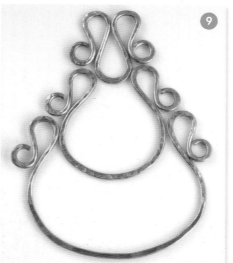. Aim not to hammer the entire piece flat, but instead facet it.

12 When you forge, the metal moves, which changes the overall shape of the wire. Arrange the tiers in position again and adjust them all so that the forms touch and all the loops are closed.

GYPSY WIRE WRAP

Each of the frames gets embellished using a gypsy wire wrap that incorporates loops from which you can hang dangles later.

· ·

Tip: I borrowed this wrap from traditional basketry. Its figure-eight path hides the wire when binding two pieces of framework together. I first taught this wrap in a project named Gypsy Wire Earrings, and because I use this method all the time, this is the name I ended up giving to the technique, too.

· ·

13 Mark each frame to indicate where the loops will go, as follows: the top tier three times, with one at the center and two marks evenly spaced at either side of it. Mark the center of the middle tier five times, and the bottom tier seven times 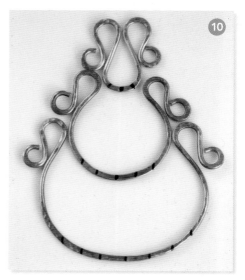.

14 First you'll wrap the bottom tier. Cut 30 inches (76.2 cm) of 24-gauge wire. Place it below one of the exterior loops, with roughly the last 2 inches (5.1 cm) pointing toward you; this sets you up to wrap away from yourself.

15 Wrap until you reach the first mark. As shown in **11**, place one jaw of the round-nose pliers below and against the tier. With the forefinger of your left hand, bring the wrapping wire around the pliers in the direction opposite the one you were wrapping, forming a loop that rests against the tier **12**. Pull the wire around the framework, remove the pliers, and you're in position to keep wrapping in the same direction as before **13**.

· ·

Tip: I use the marks as a reminder to make a loop, but when I reach that spot during the wrapping process, I use my judgment as to where exactly to place the loop.

· ·

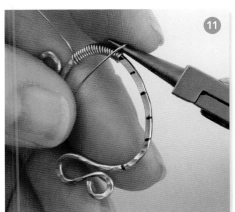

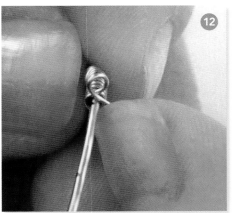

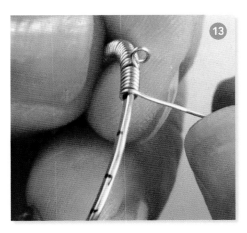

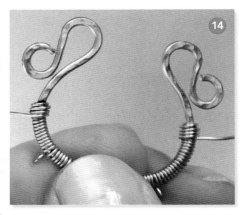

16 Repeat step 15 until you've made all of the gypsy wire wraps, then coil up the second side of the tier until you reach the exterior loops. At both ends of the wrap, go back over the initial wrap three times . Trim in the back.

17 Using 24 inches (61 cm) of 24-gauge wire for the middle tier and 7 inches (17.8 cm) for the top tier, wrap them as already described .

TRIANGLE CONNECTOR

Cut 1½ inches (3.8 cm) of 16-gauge wire. Bend it at the center with chain-nose pliers, to form a V. As shown in , roll in both ends, working halfway up the round-nose pliers, to form loops. Hammer the top and the bottom.

PADDLES

18 Cut two pieces of 16-gauge wire, each 1 inch (2.5 cm) long, flush-cutting all ends. Cut four pieces of the same wire, each ¾ inch (1.9 cm) long, making sure all ends are cut flush.

19 Forge a paddle on one end of each of the six pieces of wire. On the other end of each wire, make an eye pin that's perpendicular to the plane of the paddle, using the bottom quarter of the pliers 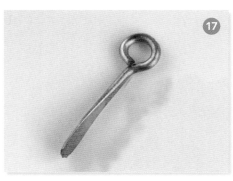. File off any burrs.

ASSEMBLE

20 Refer to (18) as you do steps 20 to 23. Connect the tiers to each other using 4-mm jump rings. Connect the triangle top to the top tier with two 4-mm jump rings. Attach the 6-mm jump ring to the center of the triangle connector. Attach the paddles to the bottom tier.

21 Antique the piece and clean it up.

22 Cut 15 pieces of 24-gauge wire, each 3 inches (7.6 cm) long, and use them to make balled head pins. Quench them in water immediately to keep the heads nice and pink (19).

23 Add one bead to each head pin and attach one to each of the loops made on the tiers, finishing them off with a wrapped eye loop with spiral cap.

VARIATION

These earrings were made with a smaller gauge of wire, and the tiers were scaled down. With just a slight alteration to the design, you've got a spectacular pair of earrings.

CAGE IT

by Tracy Stanley — Shells, rocks, cabochons, even large buttons—you can make this pendant with just about anything. It's a great opportunity to incorporate any favorite treasures that don't have holes.

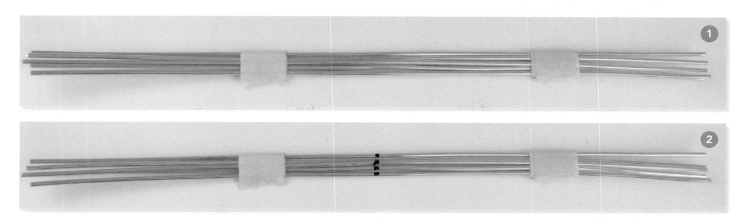

YOU'LL NEED

16-gauge dead-soft silver wire*

16 inches (40.6 cm) of 18-gauge dead-soft silver wire

3 to 5 feet (0.9 to 1.5 m) of 24-gauge dead-soft silver wire

1 inch (2.5 cm) of 14-gauge dead-soft silver wire

1 shell or flat stone of any shape

12- to 14-mm bead**

6 to 10 pearls, beads and/or stones, 6- to 8 mm

2 spacers (optional)

6 to 10 silver balled head pins, 24-gauge

Masking tape

Liver of sulfur

Ruler

Flush wire cutters

Flat-nose pliers

Round-nose pliers

Chain-nose pliers

Permanent marker

Chasing hammer

Bench block and pad

Quantity depends on size of shell or stone; see step 1.

**Its hole should accommodate 18-gauge wire*

SPOKES FOR CAGED PIECE

1 Measure your shell at the widest point and add 5 inches (12.7 cm) to this measurement. Cut five pieces of 16-gauge wire to this length.

. . . .

Tip: Straighten the wire before you cut it. This will make it much easier to get the wires to line up in the next step.

. . . .

2 Making sure all of the wires lie parallel rather than crossing over, place them side by side. Attach them together with two pieces of masking tape on either side, leaving 1 inch (2.5 cm) in the center without tape **1**.

3 Mark the center of the wires **2**.

4 Cut a piece of 18-gauge wire 6 inches (15.2 cm) long. Using flat-nose pliers, fold it in half. Slide it over the mark at the center of the taped 16-gauge wires **3**.

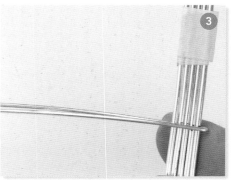

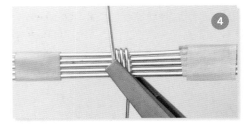

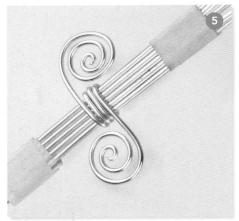

5 Bind the taped wires by folding the ends of the 18-gauge wire over the center. Fold one end of the 18-gauge and then the other for a total of three to four times around, making sure the taped wires stay flat and keeping the 18-gauge wire snug. With each turn, use the flat-nose pliers to squeeze the wires and tighten them in place 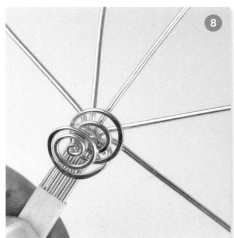.

6 Make a flat spiral on each end of the 18-gauge wire, orienting them as shown in ⑤.

7 Working on a bench block, flatten the spirals with a chasing hammer ⑥.

8 Rotate the spirals to lie over the top of the bound section ⑦. Cut 2 to 3 feet (61 to 91.4 cm) of 24-gauge wire. Keep it nearby; you'll need it after the next step.

9 Remove the masking tape from one end (and one end only!) of the bundle. Grasp one of the outside wires with the flat-nose pliers, run the tool down to the bound section, and bend the wire at a right angle. Move to the other side and repeat. Flare the other three wires in even increments, to create spokes ⑧.

10 Holding onto the bound section, remove the tape from the other end and spread the wires into spokes as you did in the previous step. **Important:** Don't let go of the piece at this point—the spokes are loose! Just move on to the next step.

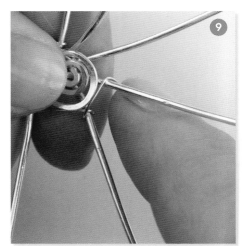

BASKET WEAVE THE SPOKES

11 Begin by wrapping the 24-gauge wire tightly around any one of the spokes two or three times.

12 Then, working away from you, wrap the 24-gauge wire over and around the next spoke . Go to the next spoke and wrap over and around it. Repeat with all of the spokes then weave a second time around them all; you should have a very stable piece at this point.

Tip: Pull the wire snug around each spoke before moving to the next section. As you move from one section to the next, make sure you like the spacing. You can adjust the angle of the spoke if not.

13 Continue to weave until the section is the size you desire 🔟. The weaving can completely cover the back of the shell or stone you plan to cage, or not. Attach the end of the weaving wire by wrapping it two to three times around the last spoke.

Tip: If you run out of weaving wire before reaching your desired size, wrap the end twice around the last spoke it reaches, then trim any extra wire off. Add more wire by attaching it around the last spoke with a double wrap, and continue on.

MAKE THE SPIRAL ARMS

14 Trim the spoke wires so there's approximately 2 inches (5.1 cm) of straight wire sticking out beyond the edges of the piece. Shape an open or closed spiral on the ends of *all but one* of the spokes. These spirals can all face the same direction, or not—that's up to you! ⑪ shows not only the orientation I chose, but also how the size of the weaving relates to the size of the shell.

Tip: After you make the first spiral, if it's too big for your taste, you can trim down the spokes.

15 The spoke that remains straight is the one your piece will hang from—the bail. Using your round-nose pliers, roll the end of the wire, creating a coil ⑫. This doesn't need to be too big, just enough to put a jump ring through it. You'll decide its exact placement after you get your shell in place.

16 Place the wirework on the block with the bail up, and use your chasing hammer to flatten and shape the spiral arms. Hammer only the spirals, not the straight parts of wire ⑬.

CAGE THE SHELL OR STONE

17 Place the shell (or stone) against the wirework (not on the side with the coiled bail) and centered in the woven area. Fold every other spiral arm up and over the shell . You can do this by hand or use flat-nose pliers to help push them in place.

Tip: As you fold the arms, check the other side to make sure the woven portion stays over the center of the shell or stone. If you like, you can fold more arms over the front, or leave them to fold over to the back.

18 Fold the remaining arms back over the weaving. These can be coiled more to fit . (This is the back of the pendant.)

19 After you're sure the fit is good, gently open the arms to take the shell out, and antique and polish the cage. (Removing the shell will keep it from getting dirty.) Replace the shell and bend the arms down in place  .

ACCENT BEAD

Using the remaining 10-inch (24.4 cm) piece of 18-gauge wire and the 12- to 14-mm bead, make a double-loop eye wrap with a spiral cap. Antique it .

JUMP RING

Using the 14-gauge wire, make a jump ring at the base of your long round-nose pliers.

EMBELLISHMENT BEADS

Make bead dangle embellishments by wire-wrapping the remaining beads (and a spacer, if desired) on the head pins  **19**. Antique them if desired.

ASSEMBLE

20 Open the jump ring and slide on the caged piece.

21 Next, slide on the embellishment beads.

22 Finally, slide on the accent bead and close the jump ring.

23 To wear the pendant, slide a cord or chain through the unused loop on the other side of the accent bead. Depending on how you decide to hang your piece, you may need to change the orientation of this loop. Do this by holding the other loop steady and turning the unused loop to the desired direction. (You can also add an optional bail to hang your pendant from if you like.)

• •

Tip: If you want to add more embellishment beads to make a bigger statement, add an additional jump ring with the extra beads.

• •

Last, but not least, get ready for the ooohs and aaahs from all who see your amazing caged piece!

VARIATION

SPIRAL WAVES RING

by Janice Berkebile Capture a focal element with spirals and basket weave to create a cool ring. Wear this fabulous piece to a cocktail party and the fun will come to you!

YOU'LL NEED

10 inches (25.4 cm) of 16-gauge sterling silver wire

18 inches (45.7 cm) of 18-gauge sterling silver wire

3 feet (91.4 cm) of 24-gauge sterling silver wire

1 large focal element, 25 to 35 mm across*

Liver of sulfur

Ring sizer

Wooden ring mandrel

Flush cutters

Round-nose pliers

Flat-nose pliers

Chain-nose pliers

Chasing hammer

Bench block and pad

Metal ring mandrel (optional)

No hole required—you can use a shell, a piece of glass, even a large cabochon. See page 106.

RING SHANK

1 Determine the size of your finger using the ring sizer ❶.

· ·

Tip: With this project, you can antique either before or after making the ring. As shown here, I oxidized all the wire before I started.

· ·

2 Place the center of the 16-gauge wire on the wooden ring mandrel on a spot one to two sizes smaller than the desired finished size. (It will be easier to enlarge the shank later than to make it smaller. Coiled wire, which is springier than wrapped wire, will be easier to adjust for fit later.) Wrap the wire twice around the mandrel ❷.

WAVE WIRES

3 Cut four pieces of 18-gauge wire, each 4½ inches (11.4 cm) long.

4 Grasp one wire with the bottom quarter of the round-nose pliers, ¼ inch (6 mm) to the right of the center of the wire ❸. Roll the wire around the tool to create a small loop in the center ❹.

5 Repeat with the remaining three wires ❺.

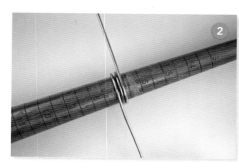

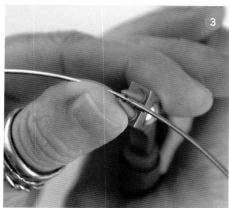

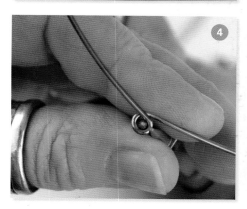

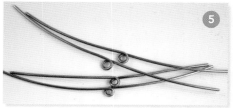

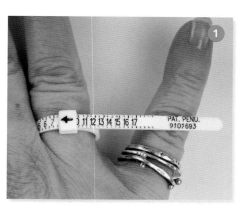

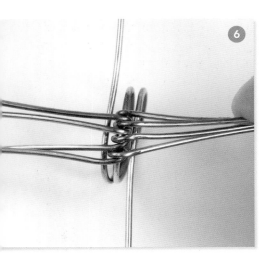

ASSEMBLE

6 Slide each of the four wave wires onto the ring shank and position them side by side on the central wrap of wire **6**.

7 Using chain-nose pliers, squeeze the loop of the wave wires so they grip tightly to the shank **7**.

8 Re-form the shank on the mandrel and double-check the ring size. Get it as close as possible to the correct size and shape by tapping it lightly with the hammer.

SHANK WRAP

9 Using flat-nose pliers, bend one end of the shank wire across the top of the wrapped shank **8**.

10 Wrap the same wire once around the shank, using chain-nose pliers to help move it **9**.

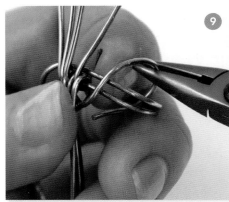

11 Bend the other end of the shank wire at a 90° angle, right next to the wave wires, and wrap once. Try to keep the shank wire tight against the wave wires as you wrap the shank.

12 Check the size of the shank; it should be correct. To finish, wrap each end of the wire two or three times around the shank.

. . . .

Tip: As you wrap the shank, if the wires twist or overlap each other, fix the placement before continuing. You may not be able to re-shape them later.

. . . .

13 To finish, crimp the wire ends down on the inside of the shank to "tell" the wires where they belong. Lift the wires back up and use flush cutters to cut the tails on the inside of the shank at an angle. Crimp the wires back in place with chain-nose pliers **10**.

WAVES AND WEAVE

14 Spread the wave wires out, keeping them perpendicular to the ring shank. Shape open spirals at each end of the wires **11**. Adjust the positioning of the wave wires as needed.

15 Place the shank with the waves upside down on the block. Using a chasing hammer, forge the wires to strengthen and facet them. Texture them with the peen end of the hammer, for a pebbly effect **12**.

16 Hold the work so the shank faces you. Wrap one end of the 24-gauge wire around any one of the wave wires, close to the shank **13**.

17 Bring the 24-gauge wire under the next wave wire and wrap it completely around that wire. Repeat to weave around all the wave wires **14** until you've used up all the 24-gauge wire. As you work, keep the weaving tight by using your thumb to press it in

toward the shank **15**. Wrap the end of the 24-gauge wire twice around the nearest wave wire and clip it on the back side, using flush cutters.

18 Dip the piece in liver of sulfur, then clean it.

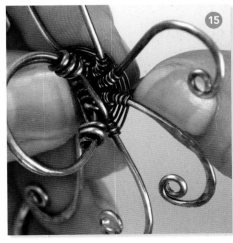

Any of these is a good choice for the focal bead.

MOUNT THE FOCAL BEAD

19 Place the focal bead face up in the center of the weave ⑯.

20 Using flat-nose pliers, bend one of the wave wires over the focal bead ⑰. Then bend the wave wire directly across from the first bent one ⑱.

21 Continue capturing the focal bead as described in step 20, bending one wave wire, then the one directly opposite it. Tighten the bends of all the wave wires to hold the focal bead firmly.

22 Once the ring is completed, try it on. If it's too small, hammer it slightly down a metal ring mandrel to increase the size. If it's slightly too large, you can re-size it by coiling 3 to 4 inches (7.6 to 10.2 cm) of 18-gauge wire around the bottom of the shank.

VARIATIONS

This design is so flexible that you can mount just about anything, including a shell, as shown in the ring at right. If the shape of your focal bead allows it, overlap and catch the spirals together, as shown in the piece at left.

ROCK AND ROLL
BY THE SEA

by Tracy Stanley

This necklace has a bit of everything in it! Make it long or make it short... whatever suits your personal style.

YOU'LL NEED

6 feet (1.8 m) of 14-gauge dead-soft sterling silver wire*

7 feet (2.1 m) of 16-gauge dead-soft sterling silver wire*

10 feet (3 m) of 18-gauge dead-soft sterling silver wire

2 feet (61 cm) of 20-gauge dead-soft sterling silver wire

Stone with drilled hole, 1 x 1¾ inches (2.5 x 4.4 cm)

Large lampwork bead, 20 mm or larger

6 or more tear-shaped pearls, 10 mm**

6 balled head pins that fit through the pearls

Small stones with holes in top (optional)

3 or more charms (optional)

Liver of sulfur

Long round-nose pliers

Chain-nose pliers

Flat-nose pliers

Flush-cut pliers

Chasing hammer

Bench block and pad

4 mandrels:

    4.5 mm diameter***

    6 mm diameter***

    10 mm diameter***

    14 mm diameter***

Large multibarrel plier (optional)

1 foot (30.5 cm) each of 16- and 14-gauge wire to use as mandrels

*The exact amount may differ depending on how long or short you choose to make your necklace

**You can use stone or glass beads of any shape instead.

***This size doesn't have to be precise.

WRAPPED STONE

1 Cut 10 inches (25.4 cm) of 16-gauge wire.

2 Run the wire through the drilled hole and make a double-loop eye wrap with spiral cap on both sides .

. . . .

Tip: If you prefer, you can use a large lampwork bead for this component.

. . . .

COILED CAGED BEAD

3 Cut a piece of 18-gauge wire 30 inches (76.2 cm) long, and a piece of 16-gauge wire 10 inches (25.4 cm) long. Coil the 18-gauge wire around the 16-gauge wire to a length of 4 inches (10.2 cm). Center the coil along the 16-gauge wire so that 3 inches (7.6 cm) of wire sticks out of each side of the coil. Make flat, tight spirals that face inward on each end of the 16-gauge wire, making sure to leave a large enough hole in the center of each spiral to poke wire through later **2**.

4 Use the chasing hammer to flatten and shape the spiraled ends.

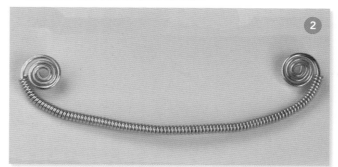

5 Hand-shape the coiled element to wrap around the large lampwork bead, with the spirals landing at either of the holes in the bead **3**.

· ·

Tip: You may need to slide out the bead, use flat-nose pliers to shape the spirals so they fit against the bead, then slide the bead back in place. If the spirals aren't tight against the bead, don't worry; the eye loop you make later will hold them down.

· ·

6 Cut 4 inches (10.2 cm) of 14-gauge wire and make an eye pin on one end **4**. (If the hole of the lampwork bead won't accommodate 14-gauge wire, cut 10 inches [25.4 cm] of 18-gauge and make a double-loop eye instead.)

7 Put a spacer on the eye pin, then slide the wire into the center of one spiral of the coiled element, through the bead, and through the other spiral of the coiled element **5**.

8 Cut the wire end to 1 inch (2.5 cm) long, and make an eye loop.

9 Forge the tops of the loops with a chasing hammer. The piece should look like **6**.

COILED JUMP RING

10 Cut a piece of 20-gauge wire 2 feet (61 cm) long. Coil it around a 14-gauge mandrel to achieve a piece 2½ inches (6.4 cm) long. Remove the mandrel.

11 Wrap 14-gauge wire around a 14-mm mandrel to make a jump ring.

12 Open the jump ring and slide on the piece you coiled in step 10. You may need to use a chain-nose pliers to move the jump ring through the coil **7**. Push it through to approximately ¼ inch (6 mm) from the end of the ring.

13 Cut the coil to fit the remaining section of jump ring. Open the ring wide enough to slip the end of the wire into the end of the coil. Close the jump ring **8** and manipulate the coil with your fingers to get the ends to meet **9**. The finished piece will look like **10**.

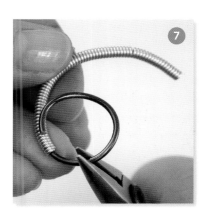

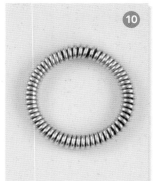

COILED EYE LINK

14 Coil 6 feet (1.8 m) of 18-gauge wire around a 16-gauge mandrel. Cut this long coil into 10 short coils, each 1 inch (2.5 cm) long. Don't forget to trim the ends!

15 Cut 25 inches (63.5 cm) of 16-gauge wire. Cut it into 10 pieces, each 2½ inches (6.4 cm) long. On one end of each, mark ¾ inch (1.9 cm) from the end of the wire, and make a loop in that part of the wire to create an eye pin 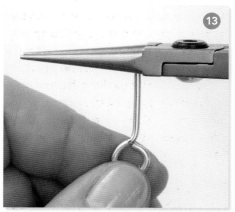.

16 Slide one of the 1-inch-long (2.5 cm) coils onto an eye pin then make a loop on the other end. Finish by using the chasing hammer to forge the top of each loop . Repeat with the remaining eye pins and coils.

PERPENDICULAR FIGURE-EIGHT LOOP

17 Cut between eight and 10 pieces of 16-gauge wire, each 1¼ inch (3.2 cm) long. Mark the center of each piece. On one end of each, employ your round-nose pliers to make an eye loop that uses half of the wire. Holding the loop between your fingers, grasp the other end of the wire with your pliers 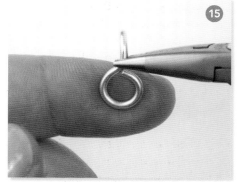, and roll the tool away to make a loop that uses the other half of the wire and is perpendicular to the first one .

18 On each twisted eye link, grasp one loop with chain-nose pliers and, with your finger on the other loop, pull it toward you ⑮. This will create an angle under the loop. Put the loop on round-nose pliers and tip and form it so its shape conforms to the tool ⑯.

19 Use the chasing hammer to forge the tops of both loops in each link ⑰.

20 Follow the same method to make perpendicular figure-eight loops out of six pieces of 14-gauge wire that have been cut into lengths of 1¾ inches (4.4 cm).

FLAT SPIRAL CHARMS

21 Cut at least three pieces (you can make more) of 16-gauge wire, each 3 inches (7.6 cm) long. Shape each one into a tightly wound spiral that has three rotations, leaving at least ½ inch (1.3 cm) of the wire straight .

22 You'll need just ½ inch (1.3 cm) to make a loop. Cut off any extra wire then make a loop on each wire that twists in a direction opposite the spirals.

23 Flatten the loops and the spirals with a chasing hammer.

JUMP RINGS

The quantities and sizes given here are approximate. Exactly how many jump rings you need of each size depends on how long you want your necklace and how long you want the tassel section to be. If you don't have a mandrel exactly the size specified, just use something close. Just make sure the jump rings are structurally sound; in other words, they must be strong enough to hold together and not twist. If you decide to use a thinner gauge of wire to make them, you can double up the rings by placing two right next to each other. I test my piece by giving it a firm tug. If the rings hold together, I'm good to go; if not, I substitute a heavier gauge or smaller rings.

- Using a 6-mm mandrel, make 40 jump rings out of 40 inches (1 m) of 14-gauge wire.

- Using a 10-mm mandrel and 1½ inches (3.8 cm) of 14-gauge wire, make one jump ring. You'll use this one for the clasp.

- Make 30 jump rings with a 4.5-mm inner diameter, using 15 inches (38.1 cm) of 16-gauge wire.

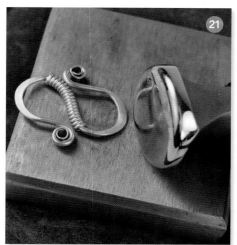

FIGURE-EIGHT CLASP

24 Cut 10 inches (25.4 cm) of 18-gauge wire. Wrap it around a 14-gauge mandrel until you've got a coil ¾ inch (1.9 cm) long.

25 Cut a piece of 14-gauge wire 5 inches (12.7 cm) long. Slide the wire into the coil, then forge the ends of it, tapering the wire to paper thin.

26 Using small round-nose pliers, make a small loop on the end of the wire. Wind the loop another rotation and a half. Flip the wire over and make the same type of loop facing the other way on the other end. Using the smallest section of the large multibarrel pliers, place one of the looped ends in the pliers (with the loop facing you) and turn the pliers away from you to form a hook. Repeat on the other side. Use a chasing hammer to forge and flatten the curves.

WIRE-WRAPPED PEARLS

Place each pearl on a head pin, then form the head pin into a wrapped eye loop with spiral cap.

. . . .

Tip: Instead of, or in addition to, the pearls, don't be afraid to use other types of beads, shells, or crystals in your piece.

. . . .

ANTIQUE THE COMPONENTS

Now's the time to antique and polish your pieces. If you have a tumbler, everything can go in except the pearls. You'll need to hand-polish those.

ASSEMBLE

27 Begin with the pendant. To attach it to the wrapped stone, use one loop of the coiled caged bead .

28 Using the other loop of the coiled caged bead, slide on the coiled jump ring . If the loop is too small to fit the coiled jump ring, or if you had to use 18-gauge wire, attach it with a jump ring.

29 Attach five of the 14-gauge jump rings to the coiled jump ring.

30 Link five 16-gauge jump rings together to make a chain, and attach them to the central 14-gauge jump ring. Attach a perpendicular figure-eight loop to the other end of the chain, and attach a 16-gauge jump ring to the other side of the perpendicular figure-eight loop . This chain should measure 2 inches (5.1 cm).

31 Randomly attach the pearls and flat spiral charms along the chain. You can also attach purchased charms and small drilled stones with jump rings and twisted eye links. Fill the chain with as many elements as you like .

32 Four jump rings remain unused on the coiled jump ring. Following the instructions in step 30, attach chains to the two jump rings closest to the

central one (the one with charms dangling from it), but make the chains 1¼ inches (3.2 cm) long instead of 2 inches (5.1 cm) long.

33 Now two jump rings remain unused on the coiled jump ring. Attach two sets each of two linked rings to these.

34 Set aside the pendant; next, you'll make the chain for the necklace. Attach the coiled eye links in a series with a 14-gauge jump ring between each one **27**.

35 Attach three linked perpendicular figure-eight loops at both ends of the chain.

36 On both ends of the chain, attach linked 14-gauge jump rings **28**. Remember, you can make this chain as long or as short as you like. Make that adjustment here with the number of jump rings you choose to use.

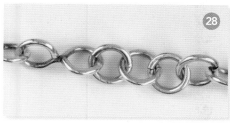

37 Attach the figure-eight clasp to one end of the chain. Attach the jump ring with the 10-mm inner diameter to the other end **29**.

38 Find the center point of the chain. Remove the 14-mm jump ring from between the coiled eye links then hang the pendant from that spot, reconnecting the whole into one long chain.

All that's left to do is to put on your necklace and strut your stuff!

VARIATION

ACORN CAPS

by Janice Berkebile

Showcase a focal bead by weaving wire caps on both ends of it to create texture. This woven pendant will fascinate everyone.

YOU'LL NEED

8 inches (20.3 cm) of 20-gauge dead-soft sterling silver wire

30 inches (76.2 cm) of 22-gauge dead-soft sterling silver wire

5 feet (1.5 m) of 24-gauge silver wire

One or two 14-gauge silver jump rings, 6 mm

Three 20-gauge silver balled head pins

1 focal bead, 1 x ½ inch (2.5 x 1.3 cm)*

3 complimentary beads, 4 to 5 mm

Liver of sulfur

Flush wire cutters

Ruler

Round-nose pliers

Chain-nose pliers

Bead reamer

*Its hole should accommodate at least 14-gauge wire. The hole may still need to be opened up with a bead reamer.

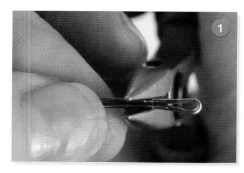

You can make all kinds of fun modifications to this design. Steps 1 through 9 tell you how to make the simplest version of this pendant (which is shown in ⑪), then the sections called Finish the Bottom explain options for altering the look. (And you can see more in Variations.) I suggest you read all the instructions completely through before you begin; decide what you want your pendant to look like, then pick and choose which instructions to follow.

ANCHOR WIRES

1 Cut two pieces of 20-gauge wire, each 4 inches (10.2 cm) long.

2 Bend both pieces of wire in half so each resembles a bobby pin ①.

3 Slide one shaped wire into the other then crimp the intersection with the chain-nose pliers ②, to allow the paired wires to fit through the hole of the focal bead ③.

4 Bend the pieces of wire coming out of each end at 90° angles to the bead and in opposite directions to each other ④.

SPOKES

5 Cut five pieces of 22-gauge wire, each 3 inches (7.6 cm) long.

6 Center the bundle of five pieces over one end of the bead ⑤. Wrap one anchor wire tightly around the bundle ⑥. Wrap the second anchor wire over the bundle in the opposite direction, staying as close as possible to the bead.

7 Form spirals on both ends of the anchor wires ⑦. This end will be the top of the pendant.

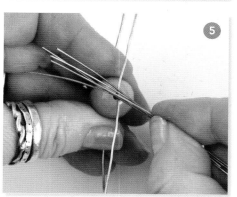

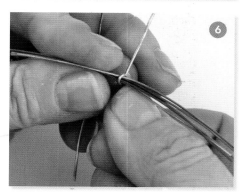

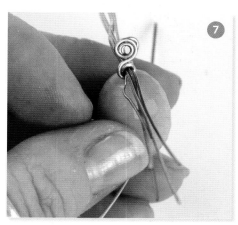

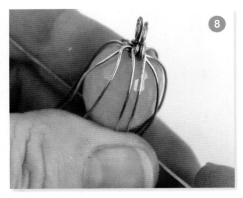

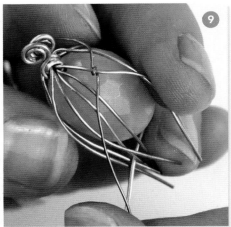

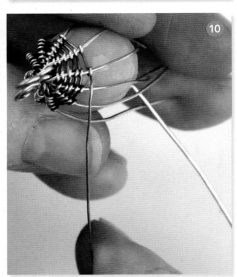

BASKET WEAVE

8 Spread the spokes evenly and shape them around the bead .

9 Cut one piece of 24-gauge wire 2½ feet (76.2 cm) long. Hold it in a way that will allow you to weave it clockwise around the bead. Leaving a ½-inch (1.3 cm) tail, wind one end under and around a spoke **9** then push it as close as possible to the spiraled anchor wires.

Bring the wire underneath the next spoke over, wrap around it once, then move on to the next spoke and repeat. Continue in this manner, maintaining tension so the basket weave looks neat, making sure the ribs are outside the spokes **10**. Continue until you're satisfied with the amount of basket-weave cap. To finish, wrap the 24-gauge wire a second time on the last spoke and trim the weaving wire close to the bead.

FINISH THE BOTTOM

You have a number of options here. You could repeat steps 5 through 7, but instead of a bundle of five 22-gauge wires, use just one. Wrap it with the anchor wires, then spiral the ends of the anchor wires and each end of the spoke, as shown in **11**. Add a 14-gauge silver jump ring to the top, connecting it through the spirals. Antique the finished piece.

Or you could repeat steps 5 through 9 on the other side of the bead, then create fancy spirals on both of the

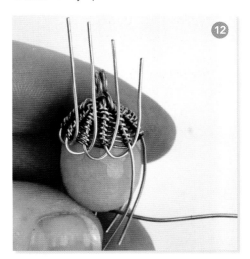

woven sides by bringing the end of each spoke across to the next spoke and sliding it underneath ⑫. Tug on the end of each wire to make a consistent curve, then trim all the spoke wires to the same length. Form the ends into spiral shapes ⑬ then seat them into position ⑭. (Note that the pendant shown on page 114 has these fancy, interlocked spirals capping both sides of the bead.) Add a jump ring to the top and the bottom of the finished piece, connecting each through the spirals. Add three wrapped eye loops with beads to the bottom jump ring. Antique the finished piece.

VARIATION

⑮ shows spirals that extend beyond the lower portion of the basket weave, as well as a single, more complex dangle than described in these instructions. As shown in ⑯, this capping technique was used not only to make a pendant but also to embellish the beads in the necklace. In ⑰, the brown bead flanked by amber beads has an upper section of basket weave perched at a jaunty angle because of the way the hole was drilled. And ⑱ shows how when you change the proportion of basket weave to bead size, you can achieve different looks.

WIRE POD

by Janice Berkebile

As you weave this organic wire pod, it takes on its own personality. Make several, fill them with your favorite beads, and wear them together. Get back to nature as you listen to the gentle rhythm of the pods knocking together!

YOU'LL NEED

18 inches (45.7 cm) of 18-gauge bronze wire

6 feet (1.8 m) of 24-gauge copper wire

An assortment of 12 to 20 beads*

Liver of sulfur

Ruler

Large-gauge flush wire cutters

Round-nose pliers

Chain-nose pliers

Long round-nose pliers

Chasing hammer

Bench block and pad

Choose complementary beads, such as a variety of shells, pearls, and semiprecious stones.

FRAME

. . . .

Tip: Reminder! Use large-gauge flush wire cutters to cut the bronze wire; it's hard stuff and feels two gauges heavier than it really is.

. . . .

1 Cut the bronze wire exactly in half; these pieces will serve as the frames. The copper wire will be the weaving wire. Hold one of the pieces of framing (bronze) wire horizontally in front of you. Place the weaving (copper) wire across it, with a 1-inch (2.5 cm) tail of wire facing toward you. Coiling it away from yourself, wrap the weaving wire once around the framing wire ❶.

2 Place the second piece of framing wire vertically over the first. You now need to secure the framing wires to each other. Using the weaving wire, wrap to the left of, and under, the next piece of framing wire. Bring the wire up and over that framing wire to secure it. Move on to the next framing wire and wrap, repeating until there's a wrap around each of the four spokes ❷. Weave one more row as shown in ❸. This area will be the bottom of the finished pod.

3 Slide one of the framing wires down—not out—so you can access the center of the framing wire. At its center, bend the framing wire roughly 90° with the chain-nose pliers ❹. Slide the weaving wire up and over the bend.

Repeat this process with the other piece of the framing wire. You've now bent spines into the frame and created the point at the bottom of the finished pod.

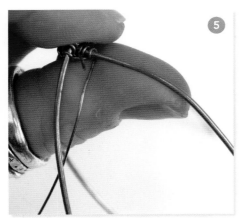

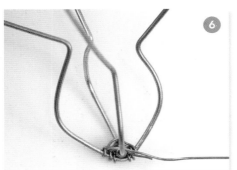

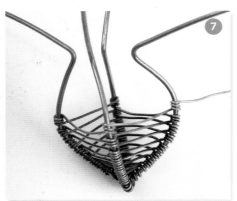

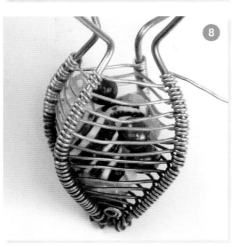

BASKET WEAVE

The tail of the weaving wire should be poking out of the bottom of the pod. Use this as a reference as you begin weaving. I start the weaving process looking at the exterior of the bottom. Make sure to bring the wires *under* the spines as you weave.

4 Continue to wrap the weaving wire underneath and around each spine then move on to wrap the next spine. After three or four rounds, the piece will begin to feel stable. Stop wrapping.

5 Use your thumb to create a bulbous shape about 1 inch (2.5 cm) tall out of each of the spines **5**. Define the neck by bending the wires so the four spines come together in the center and the ends of the wires point out **6**.

6 Antique the wire. Continue to basket weave your way around the spines, but now coil *three* times around each spine before moving on to the next one **7**. This will open up the space between each weaving wire so the beads you'll place inside later will show more. As you progress, constantly manipulate the wires to maintain the form.

After you weave your way past the widest point of the framing, the weaving wire will begin to slip. Keep it in place with your finger, as you weave, to avoid large gaps.

7 About three-quarters of the way up the frame, stop weaving. Place the beads inside the basket weaving **8**. Weave a few more rows, coiling around each spine three times; finish the weave with one wrap around each spine for a couple of rows.

. . . .

Tip: Stuff the pod completely full, or leave a little room so the beads can roll and click inside.

. . . .

8 To close the pod, bend the spines close together at the neck. Weave around the spines, closing the hole tightly so the beads don't fall out **9**. Coil the leftover weaving wire around one of the remaining spines—but *not* the longest one **10**.

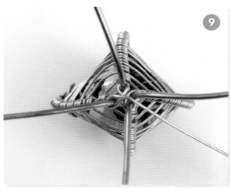

BAIL

9 The bail is made from the longest of the four spines. Working three-quarters of the way from the tip of the long round-nose pliers, make a double loop that's seated at the top and center of the pod ⑪. *Don't* cut off the remaining wire; instead, coil it around the top of the pod, across a spine or two ⑫, and finish it off as a tendril or a spiral. Make a spiral or a tendril to finish the wire of the spine with the coiled wire.

MAKING TENDRILS

Hammer the end of the wire into a paddle ⑬. Grip the tip of the paddle with the tip of the long round-nose pliers ⑭, then rotate the tool away from you. Reposition your hand and keep winding the wire up the pliers to create a tendril that's tighter at the end and wider closer to the bail ⑮.

10 Finish each of the remaining spines as either tendril or a spiral.

11 To finish the tail, cut it to about ¾ inch (1.9 cm) long. Spiral it in and tuck it between two of the spines at the bottom of the pod ⑯. (This can actually be done anytime after the pod is started.)

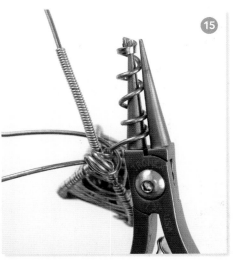

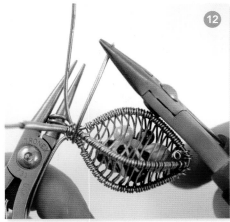

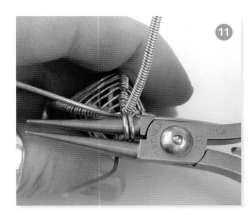

CASCADING SPIRALS BRACELET

by Tracy Stanley

Spirals, spirals, and more spirals…here's a pretty bracelet that will make you a real expert when it comes to forming this shape.

YOU'LL NEED

4 feet (1.2 m) of 18-gauge dead-soft copper wire

4½ feet (1.4 m) of 14-gauge dead-soft copper wire

15 feet (4.6 m) of 24-gauge dead-soft copper wire

Twenty 14-gauge copper jump rings, 6.5 to 7 mm

One 14-gauge copper jump ring, 9 mm

Beads*

Liver of sulfur

Mandrel, 3.5 mm in diameter

Flush wire cutters

Ruler

Marker

Small round-nose pliers

Flat-nose pliers

Chain-nose pliers

Chasing hammer

Bench block and pad

*See the tip box below

Tip: It's up to you what beads to use to embellish! Small bicone crystals, pearls, gemstones—even glass seed beads will work. How many you'll need will depend on their size; I recommend 3-mm beads. You'll need enough to cover the front side of the coils completely.

LINKS

1 Coil all the 18-gauge wire around the mandrel. Remove the coil from the mandrel and cut it into ½-inch (1.3 cm) sections, trimming each end with the flush wire cutters 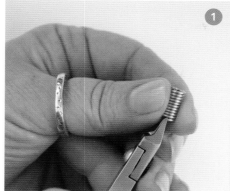. Set aside.

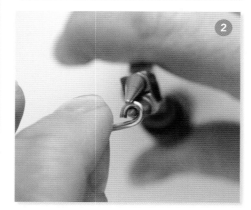

2 Cut two pieces of 14-gauge wire, each 4 inches (10.2 cm) long. Mark the end of each one 1¾ inches (4.4 cm) from one end.

3 Set one piece of wire aside. Using the round-nose pliers, make a loop on the marked end of the wire **2**. (If the loop is too large for your taste, use flat-nose pliers to squeeze it and make it smaller **3**.)

Tip: This bracelet can be made out of silver wire instead, or you can even try a combination of both copper and silver!

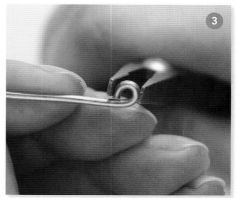

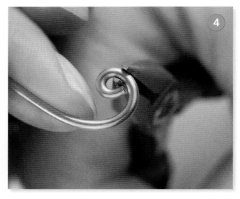

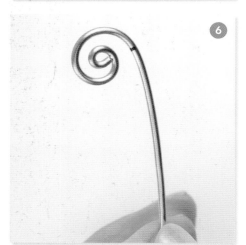

4 Hold the inside of the loop with chain-nose pliers, and use your other hand to begin to form an open spiral by pulling the wire around ④. When you've turned as far as you can, re-position the pliers ⑤ and repeat until you've reached the mark you made on the wire ⑥.

• •

Tip: The secret to making a nice smooth spiral is keeping the chain-nose pliers in a fully curved section as you form. If you grasp the wire too close to the area you're forming, it will get unwanted kinks in it. You can decide how much space you want between the turns. All you need is enough room for the tip of the pliers.

• •

5 Repeat steps 3 and 4 with the second piece of wire. Orienting the spirals in opposite directions and using your chasing hammer, flatten each spiral up to the mark ⑦.

6 Insert both of the spiraled wires into any one of the ½-inch (1.3 cm) sections of coil ⑧. Use round-nose pliers to make a loop on one of the ends of wire ⑨. Form the rest of that wire into an open spiral ⑩. Repeat on the other wire ⑪.

7 Forge the spirals made in step 6, making sure not to hit the coil ⑫.

8 Using chain-nose pliers, squeeze down the end of the coil wire to hold both spiraled wires in this link more tightly together ⑬. There will still be some movement, but that's okay.

9 Repeat steps 2 through 8 to make a total of five links. Antique them, as well as the jump rings. Clean them up with polishing pads or tumble them.

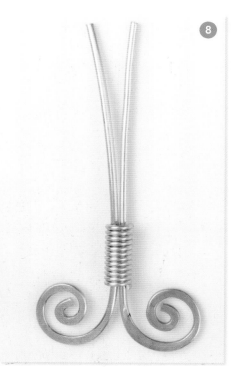

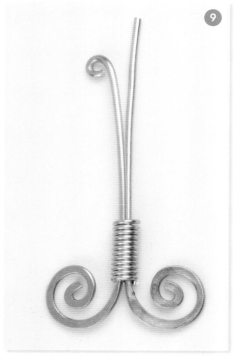

EMBELLISH

10 Cut 2 feet (61 cm) of 24-gauge wire, antique it, and wrap it three times around the end of one of the coils binding a link. Slide on three beads, position them on the front side of the coil, and pull the wire around the back and then to the front .

11 Pull the wire hard, so it slides between the coils on the back side .

12 Continue attaching beads to the front of the coil and wrapping around until you've covered the front with beads .

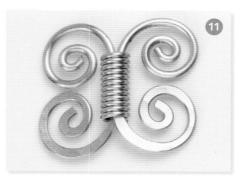

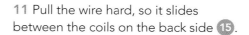

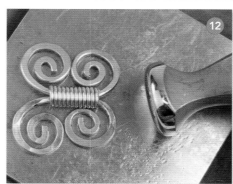

13 Wind this wire three times around where the spiraled wires come out of the coiled section. Trim the wire to approximately 3 inches (7.6 cm). Using chain-nose pliers, insert this wire into the center of the coil . If it'll go all the way through, pull it tight and trim off; if it won't go through, trim the wire short and tuck it into the end of the coil. Finish off the other end in the same way (most of the time it won't fit all the way through).

14 Embellish the other four links in the same way.

CLASP

You can choose from the many clasps shown in this book. I like the spiral clasp **18** because it has a shape similar to the links. Instructions for this clasp are given in the Coils and Beads Bracelet project (page 80). Don't forget to antique it.

ASSEMBLE

15 Antique the jump rings. Connect the links sequentially, using pairs of the small jump rings **19**.

16 Use two small jump rings to attach the clasp to one end, as shown in **20**.

17 Attach the 9-mm jump ring to the other end, using two small jump rings **21**.

. . . .

Tip: You can make the bracelet longer by adding more 9-mm jump rings at the end, linked in a chain with 6.5-mm jump rings.

. . . .

Now put on this fabulous bracelet. You'll see it's not only a showstopper, but so comfortable to wear!

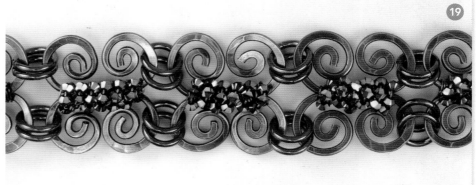

BLOOM!

by Janice Berkebile

Bend, weave, and coil wire to create a frame
for the perfect focal bead. Everyone who sees
this dynamic blossom pendant will love it.

YOU'LL NEED

3½ feet (1 m) of 18-gauge dead-soft copper wire

6 feet (1.8 m) of 24-gauge dead-soft copper wire

2½ feet (76.2 cm) of 16-gauge dead-soft copper wire

2 feet (61 cm) of 22-gauge dead-soft copper wire

1 focal bead, 15 to 25-mm rondelle or flat bead*

Liver of sulfur

Round-nose pliers

Ruler

Marker

Chain-nose pliers

Flush wire cutters

Long round-nose pliers

Chasing hammer

Bench block and pad

Small horn anvil

Measuring tape

The hole should accommodate 16-gauge wire. Also see the box on page 132.

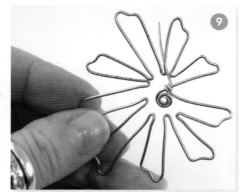

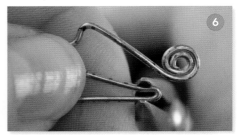

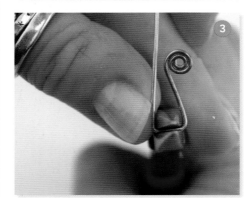

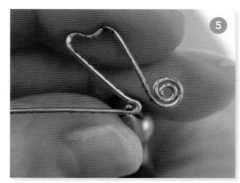

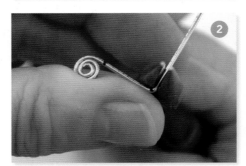

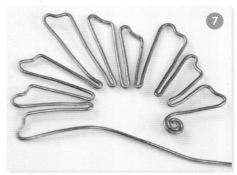

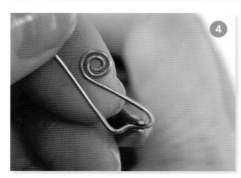

FRAME

1 You'll start by making the center of the frame. At one end of the 18-gauge wire, make a spiral with two full revolutions, leaving the hole large enough for 16-gauge wire to pass through ①.

2 Next, you'll form the first petal. Measure ½ inch (1.3 cm) along the wire from where the spiral ends. At the marked spot, use chain-nose pliers to make a crisp bend in the wire in a direction opposite the spiral **2**.

3 The top of the petal is the width of the chain-nose pliers. Make another crisp angle to bring the wire up on the other side of the petal **3**.

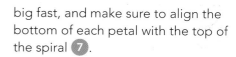

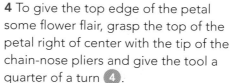

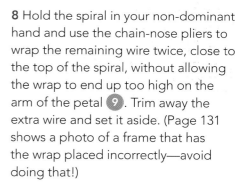

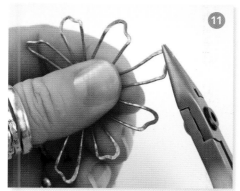

4 To give the top edge of the petal some flower flair, grasp the top of the petal right of center with the tip of the chain-nose pliers and give the tool a quarter of a turn **4**.

5 To begin the second petal, grasp the wire in the tip of the chain-nose pliers and make a sharp angle, as shown in **5**. Squeeze this angle into a sharp V, but don't close the space at the end of the wires **6**. (The space will be needed later for the basket weave. See page 131 for a photo of a frame that's been shaped incorrectly—and avoid doing that.)

6 Make a total of nine petals along the 18-gauge wire, varying the length of each slightly so some are longer and some shorter than the previous one. Make sure to control the length of each petal, however, as it can get big fast, and make sure to align the bottom of each petal with the top of the spiral **7**.

7 Bend the framework into a circle and trim the end of the wire to 2 inches (5.1 cm). Undo a little of the spiral. Place the end of the wire behind the spiral and just above it **8**.

8 Hold the spiral in your non-dominant hand and use the chain-nose pliers to wrap the remaining wire twice, close to the top of the spiral, without allowing the wrap to end up too high on the arm of the petal **9**. Trim away the extra wire and set it aside. (Page 131 shows a photo of a frame that has the wrap placed incorrectly—avoid doing that!)

9 Position the spiral in the center of the frame and finesse the form of the frame. Forge the ends of the petals and texture them, if desired **10**. Give the petals some dimension by using the chain-nose pliers to bend them **11**.

10 Using the leftover wire you trimmed off in step 8, follow steps 1 through 9 to make a second frame about ½ inch (1.3 cm) smaller or larger in diameter than the first frame; antique them both **12**.

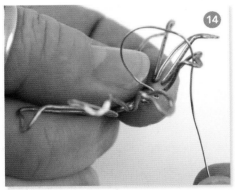

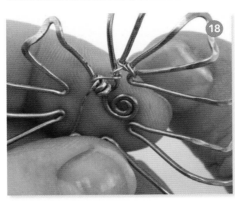

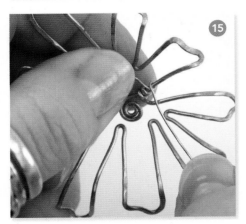

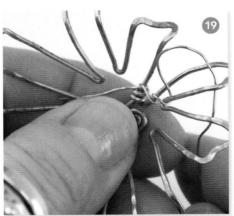

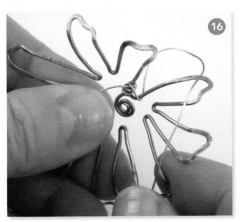

BASKET WEAVE

11 For the basket weave, each frame will require 3 feet (91.4 cm) of weaving wire, so cut the 24-gauge wire in half. Anchor the tail of the weaving wire above the wire wrap, in the direction shown in **13**. (The wire that's showing is the tail; the working wire is hidden behind the thumb.)

12 Wrap the weaving wire around the frame wire and up through the petal.

. . . .

Tip: Instead of poking the tail of the weaving wire up though the petals each time, make a loose loop out of the weaving wire and push it through **14**. Then you can pull the rest of the wire through the small space without kinking it.

. . . .

13 The weaving wire will bridge the gap between two petals. As shown in **15**, **16**, **17**, **18**, and **19**, pull the weaving wire from the wire of one petal and over to the closer side of the next petal. Pull the wire across and push a loose loop of wire down through the petal. Wrap up, over, and across the petal. Pull the wire down on the second side and push a loose loop up through the petal. As you work around the frame for the first row, you should draw the base of each petal closer to its neighbor. Continue in this fashion to complete the first row of basket weave.

14 After the first row, adjust the petals so they're equally spaced. Continue to basket weave **20** until you run out of wire. To secure the end of the wire, wrap it twice around the last wire and trim it in back. Move the spiral to the center and adjust the petals.

15 Weave the other frame in the same fashion. Set both frames aside.

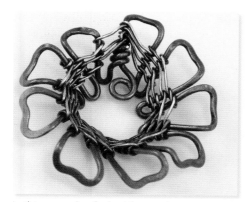

In this example of a bad frame, the wrap holding the frame secure is too high, and it therefore positions the basket weave high on that petal. In addition, the Vs that create the petal bottoms are too rounded. The solution: Squeeze them gently to make the Vs sharper, but don't close them.

SPIRAL HEAD PIN

16 Two inches (5.1 cm) from one end of the 16-gauge wire, make a 90° bend. Place the round-nose pliers in the crook of the bend with the short end of the wire at 90° to the tip of the pliers. Place your forefinger on the wire to hold it in place. Start to form a spiral on the very tip of the tool by pushing the wire with your thumb **21** so it takes the shape of the pliers **22**.

17 With that initial circle formed, use the chain-nose pliers to form a spiral, making it a little more than two full revolutions. Trim the wire at an angle **23**.

18 Place the other end of the wire—which will be called the stem wire from now on—down through the hole of a small horn anvil. Hammer the very end of the spiral to form a paddle. Hammer the rest of the spiral to strengthen it. Texture it with the peen side of hammer. File the paddle if necessary **24**.

19 Poke the round-nose pliers up through the center hole to pooch out the spiral **25**. That way, when it's placed over the bead during assembly, it will fit better. Your piece should look like **26**.

20 Wrap the 22-gauge wire around the stem wire to create a coil about 2½ inches (6.4 cm) long. Remove the coil.

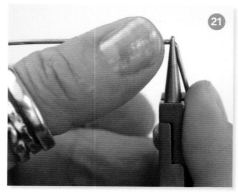

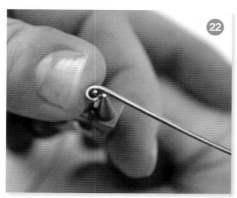

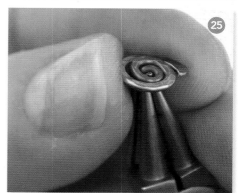

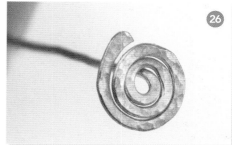

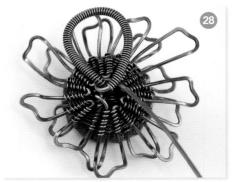

ASSEMBLE

21 Form both frames up around the focal bead so the bead nests inside them. Antique all of the wire parts in liver of sulphur, then clean them up.

22 Place the stem wire down through the focal bead and through the spiral of both of the framework pieces, then slide the coil onto the stem wire 27.

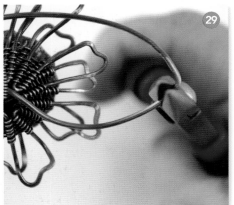

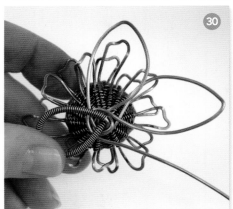

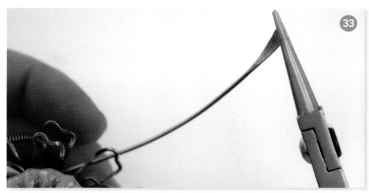

CHOOSING A FOCAL BEAD

Select a group of potential beads, all with 16-gauge holes. Rondelle or flat beads with a hole in the center are great for this project, but you can also try lampwork beads, pebbles, and enameled beads. "Interview" each bead, mounting it temporarily with the spiral head pin and the framework, to see how it will really look.

23 To make the bail, bend the coil around until the two ends meet. Wrap the stem wire once behind the bail to secure it (28).

LEAVES

24 Use your fingers and chain-nose pliers to shape the stem wire into the rough outline of a leaf (29). Secure it by wrapping the wire in between the framework and the bail. Form a second leaf, again securing it in the back (30).

25 Hammer the leaves to strengthen and texturize them (31).

TENDRILS

26 Wrap the stem wire once more around to secure it; you'll use the rest as a tendril. Cut it to 3 inches (7.6 cm) long. Hammer the very end of the wire attached to the leaves

into a paddle. Trim the cut-off wire to 6 inches (15.2 cm) long and paddle both ends (32).

27 Grasp the paddled end of the wire attached to the leaves in the long round-nose pliers (33), and curl the wire up the tool to create a tendril (34).

28 Slide the cut-off wire with the paddled ends between the framework and the leaves (35), and wrap it once around the base of the bail to secure it (36). This takes up some slack and tightens the piece. Curl both ends to shape them into tendrils. Adjust the leaves and tendrils as desired.

VARIATION

1

2

3

5

6

1 RENÉE CORRY
SSSERPENTINE BANGLE, 2004
1.7 x 7 x 0.3 cm
Sterling silver wire, faceted garnet
beads; oxidized
Photo by Lane L. Corry

2 LISA NIVEN KELLY
WIRE SHOWCASE, 2008
41 x 2 cm
Sterling silver wire, crystal beads, handmade
glass beads; spiraled, coiled, woven, braided,
forged, oxidized
Photo by artist

3 JANICE BERKEBILE
MIDNIGHT LANTERN, 2011
Pendant, 4¼ inches (10.8 cm) long
Sterling silver wire and charms,
lampwork beads, enameled beads;
basket weave, wirework
Photo by Stewart O'Shields

4 ROSANNE B. COX
UNTITLED, 2010
Largest bead, 1.4 x 1.4 x 1 cm
Sterling silver wire, handmade glass bead
Photo by Lisa J. Goodman

5 CHERYL SWEENEY
ANTIQUE IVORY VIKING BRACELET, 2011
2.4 x 7.7 x 7.1 cm
Sterling silver wire, handmade glass beads
Photo by artist

6 TRACY STANLEY
WILD AND CRAZY BRACELET, 2011
3½ inches (8.9 cm) in diameter
Sterling silver wire, sterling silver beads; coiled
Photo by Stewart O'Shields

1

3

1 TRACY STANLEY
CAGE IT PENDANT WITH KUCHI COIL BEADS, 2011
Chain, 24½ inches (62.2 cm) long;
pendant, 4 inches (10.2 cm) long
Sterling silver wire, stone pendant, smoky quartz beads; coiled, hand made
Photo by Stewart O'Shields

2 MARY ANN D'AMICO
MERMAID'S TREASURE OMEGA NECKLACE, 2010
9.5 x 5 x 1.3 cm
Sterling silver wire, semiprecious gemstones, freshwater pearls, crystals, silver Bali beads; forged, formed, wire wrapped, oxidized, hand polished
Photo by artist

3 KIMBALL OTTERBEIN
GREEN GARNET TASSEL, 2009
91.4 x 6.4 cm
Copper wire, green garnet, glass beads, jasper, recycled glass flowers
Photo by Kathy Brughelli

4 JANICE BERKEBILE
MOULIN ROUGE, 2006
10 x 4 inches (25.4 x 10.2 cm)
Sterling silver wire and caps, rubies; basket weave, wirework
Photo by Stewart O'Shields

5 LAURA GADZIK
ALAINA NECKLACE, 2009
3.8 x 1.9 x 1 cm
Sterling silver wire, sterling silver chain, freshwater pearls, fluorite; wire wrapped, basket weave, oxidized
Photo by artist

6 JANICE BERKEBILE
BLEEDING HEART LINK BRACELET, 2011
7½ inches (19 cm) long
Sterling silver wire; wirework
Photo by Stewart O'Shields

4

5

6

1

2

1 TRACY STANLEY
ENCRUSTED NECKLACE, 2011

9 x 5 inches (22.9 x 12.7 cm)
Sterling silver wire, pearls, stone beads, shell
beads, crystal beads
Photo by Stewart O'Shields

2 TRACY STANLEY
*VIKING KNIT AND KESHI PEARL
NECKLACE*, 2005

21 inches (53.3 cm) long
Sterling silver wire, keshi pearls, freshwater
pearls, bronze cones; Viking knit, hand made
Photo by Stewart O'Shields

3 JANICE BERKEBILE
WOVEN SHELL JEWEL, 2011

Pendant, 4¼ inches (10.8 cm) long
Sterling silver wire and charms, shells, pearls;
basket weave, wirework
Photo by Stewart O'Shields

4 JANICE BERKEBILE
POD RINGS, 2006

Tallest, 2 inches (5.1 cm)
Lampwork beads, semiprecious beads,
sterling silver wire, beads, pearls;
basket weave, wirework
Photo by Stewart O'Shields

5 TRACY STANLEY
EGYPTIAN COIL BRACELET, 2000

7½ inches (19 cm) long
Sterling silver wire
Photo by Stewart O'Shields

6 TRACY STANLEY
CASCADING SPIRALS BRACELET, 2011

7¾ inches (19.7 cm) long
Sterling silver wire, sterling silver tubing,
sterling silver charms
Photo by Stewart O'Shields

7 JANICE BERKEBILE
MOULIN ROUGE, 2006

10 x 4 inches (25.4 x 10.2 cm)
Sterling silver wire, Peruvian blue opal,
gaspeite; basket weave, Viking knit, wirework
Photo by Stewart O'Shields

3

4

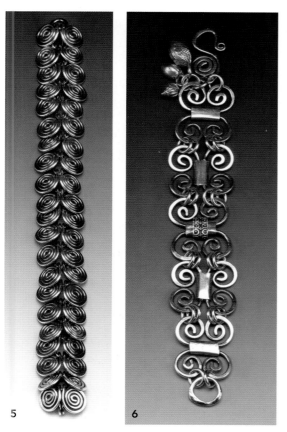

5   6

7

1

2

1 TRACY STANLEY
SHE LOVES IT AT THE BEACH—
CHAIN AND BEAD BRACELET, 2007
8 inches (20.3 cm) long
Sterling silver wire, shells, pearls, cubic zirco-
nias, quartz, rubies, hematite, bronze lentil
beads; wire wrapped, hand made
Photo by Stewart O'Shields

2 JANICE BERKEBILE
TAHITIAN DAISY, 2007
Chain, 18 inches (45.7 cm) long; pendant, 1¼ inches
(3.2 cm) long
Sterling silver wire, Tahitian pearls; wirework
Photo by Stewart O'Shields

3 TRACY STANLEY
SHELL PENDANT NECKLACE, 2008
Chain, 28 inches (71.1 cm) long; pendant, 6¼ inches
(15.9 cm) long
Sterling silver wire, shell, lampworked bead
by Kristina Logan, freshwater pearls, smoky
quartz beads, hematite beads; Byzantine chain
technique, hand made
Photo by Stewart O'Shields

4 JANICE BERKEBILE
TAHITIAN TEAR DROP, 2005
18 inches (45.7 cm) long
Sterling silver wire caps, Tahitian pearls; wirework
Photo by Stewart O'Shields

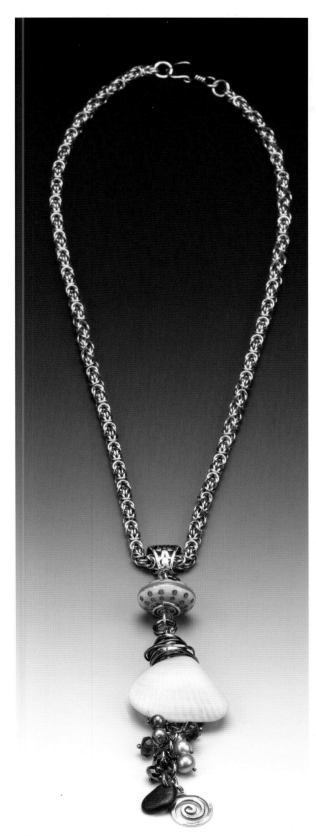

3

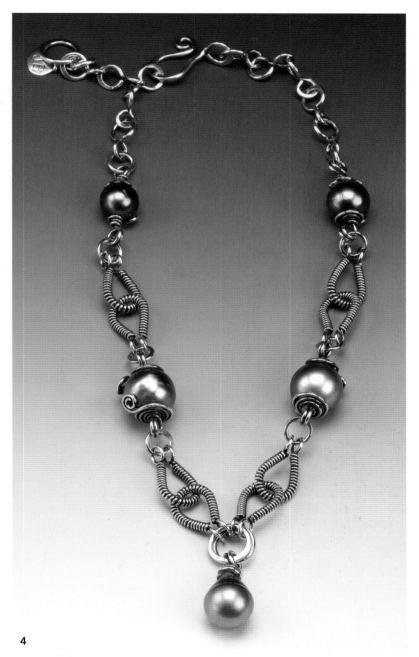

4

ABOUT THE AUTHORS

Janice Berkebile and Tracy Stanley met when they worked together at a bead store in Bellevue, Washington. They partnered to form Wired Arts, a business that offers wire-working classes and sells tools, in 2006. Check out their website at www.wiredarts.net.

Photo by Tracy Stanley

JANICE BERKEBILE has always been attracted to the fanciful rather than the practical. When she discovered beads, it was love. She's drawn in by the gleam, glint, and glow of their colors. Even trade beads, worn from travel and rich with history, beckon her to touch them and become part of their story. When Janice was introduced to wire, she thought, "Finally, a thread I can relate to! Strong yet malleable, and no knots!" Wire longs to wrap itself around beads, framing them and making each one special.

Janice finds the forms, textures, and architecture of plants, shells, and pods amazing. They provide her with inspiration for movement and patterns. Her focus is wire and metalwork, drawing from nature and incorporating texture and form into her work.

In 2005, Janice won first and second place in the Beaded Inspirations Wirework category at the Puget Sound Bead Festival. Her piece *It's a Mystery* took third place in the non-wearables category in the 2006 Bead Dreams competition.

Janice lives in Kirkland, Washington, where she teaches at Fusion Beads. She also teaches at bead stores from Alaska to Florida, and from Hawaii to Rhode Island; at shows including Bead Fest, Bead&Button, and BABE! (Bay Area Bead Extravaganza); at Adorn Me, Art & Soul, and other mixed-media shows; and for bead societies. She has contributed projects to various magazines. Her work has been featured in several books, including *Wrap, Stitch, Fold & Rivet* (Lark Jewelry & Beading); *Stamped Metal Jewelry*; and *Metal Style*. She teaches online classes through Beaducation.com.

Photo by Tracy Stanley

TRACY STANLEY has taught beading, wire, and metal working techniques for more than 18 years. Because she loves organic elements, she uses them as inspiration in her work. She rarely plans pieces out on paper, preferring to just let things fall together naturally, letting one thing lead to another, until the finished piece looks balanced and cohesive.

A big believer in quality tools and solid techniques, Tracy thinks learning correct techniques and bringing them into practice will make for pieces that are not only structurally sound, but also beautiful. She really enjoys teaching these skills and passing on her knowledge to students all over the country.

Tracy has lived in the beautiful Northwest her whole life, and the lovely natural surroundings have definitely influenced her style of wire and metal work. Over the years she has taught in bead stores all over the United States. She's been an instructor at workshops on the Oregon Coast, on cruise ships, and even during a trip to Italy. She currently teaches at Fusion Beads and at shows around the country, including Bead Fest, Wire Masters, Bead&Button, and the BABE! show. Her work appears in a number of books, including *500 Beaded Objects* (Lark Beading & Jewelry), *Make Stamped Metal Jewelry*, and *101 Gorgeous Earrings*, and she has contributed articles to both *Bead&Button* and *Beadwork* magazines. Tracy also has classes available online at Beaducation.com.

What's planned for the future? Hopefully more travel, more teaching, and spreading the knowledge she has about wire and metal.

ACKNOWLEDGMENTS

My adventures with wire and beads have been an extraordinary journey. Of course, I didn't travel this road alone. My family and friends have always been there supporting me from the beginning. I appreciate your always being there for me.

While working at the best bead store in the world, I discovered inspiration, a passion for wire, and friends who believed in me even when I didn't believe in myself. While that shop has since closed, the people I found there will remain family forever. I'll be forever grateful to Kathy Dannerbeck, who opened the gate and encouraged me to start teaching.

Radiating from this circle came many mentors and friends from all across the country. I'm truly grateful to each of them for giving me what I needed at just the right moment in time:

Lynne Merchant brought wirework in its contemporary form to the United States. I'm grateful to have worked with her. She taught me not only how to relate tools to wire, but to do it with integrity and to work with nothing but the best.

NanC Meinhardt was there for me when I was just getting started, and she helped me find my voice. She has taught me more than she knows!

These days, Carole Tripp and Blanche Costa keep me on track, providing sound advice and gentle encouragement.

To the staff at Lark Jewelry & Beading, and especially to my editor, Nathalie Mornu, for taking Tracy and me through the process of becoming authors. Without them, this book was all talk.

To Tracy my adopted big sister. Who knew I needed a fourth older sister?! She's a constant source of support and opinions, all served up with her unique perspective!

To all of my fur babies who keep me sane and totally entertained.

And to Jack, who grounds and sustains me, always.

—Janice

I'd like to thank the following people who were such an important part of my wire-working journey:

Kathy Dannerbeck, for encouraging me to teach and for believing and supporting me in this venture.

NanC Meinhardt, for forcing me to spread my wings and get out and teach at the national level.

Lynne Merchant, for awakening the world to a new-yet-old style of wire working and for setting such a high standard of workmanship, emphasizing quality materials and tools.

My bead-store "family," for their friendship and support.

Thank you to Carole Tripp and Blanche Costa, two women who have always supported my teaching career and given me great words of encouragement.

A big thank you to all of the students who have taken my classes over the years and allowed me to assist their wire-working experience. They've made me a better instructor with every class I teach.

Lark Jewelry & Beading, especially editor Nathalie Mornu, for guiding us through this experience and making our dream of being published come true.

Janice Berkebile, for going on this adventure with me. It's nice to have someone to share the highs and lows with!

My family, for putting up with the crazy schedule, wire flying, and hammer tapping late at night.

My sweet dog Bogey, for reminding me to take a break and breathe when times get crazy!

And finally, my Dad, who told me over and over that I should write a book. Hey, Dad, I finally did it!

—Tracy

INDEX